Another Bloody Tangle!

Another Bloody Tangle!

The trials and tribulations of an 'incomplete' angler

Peter Bishop

SPORTS
BOOKS

Published by SportsBooks Ltd

Copyright: Peter Bishop ©
August 2005

SportsBooks Limited
PO Box 422
Cheltenham
GL50 2YN
United Kingdom
Tel: 01242 256755
Fax: 01242 254694
e-mail   randall@sportsbooks.ltd.uk
Website www.sportsbooks.ltd.uk

Cover art by Martin Ursell

Typeset in Palatino LT Std

A CIP catalogue record for this book is available from the
British Library.

ISBN 1899807 28 4

Printed by Creative Print and Design, Wales

Dedication

This book is dedicated to the memory of my father, the infinitely talented John Bishop. A scientist, marine artist and model maker of some note, he taught me many things, but not the art of angling. Nevertheless, he was still the inspiration for writing this book. If my humble achievements in life ever amount to half of his I will depart this world a contented man.

Contents

Acknowledgements

This book would never have come about had it not been for the following people. Firstly, my fishing companion, and then fellow sports journalist, Garry Doolan, who suggested it as we returned home from another fishing trip littered with mishaps, and then sub-edited the first draft for me.

Then there is Ian Courtney, who taught me how to fish when we were kids and most recently helped me recall all those personalities and events that shaped my early fishing days. Likewise, my grateful thanks go to pals Mark Jones, Chris McGuinness and Ben Topham for reminding me of all the days we have shared which I would rather forget!

Work colleague John Mennie also deserves a special mention for sorting out my various computer calamities without which several chapters may have disappeared forever, and denied my publisher Randall Northam the tedious task of correcting my occasional misuse of apostrophes! Seriously, I am indebted to Randall for the faith he showed in *Another Bloody Tangle* when others hesitated.

Apart from everyone at SportsBooks, I also owe a huge debt of gratitude to my wife Maria for her enduring love, encouragement and support during the times when I hid myself away in the study.

Finally, to anyone who might be offended by anything that has been written about them, I would point out only one person emerges from the pages of this book looking foolish and that, I regret to say, is me!

Introduction

As far as I can see, angling literature falls into three basic categories. First, there are the 'where to fish' guides to help you locate the best fisheries. The second type are the often lavishly illustrated instruction manuals written by, or featuring a 'celebrity' angler, which are intended to get you started or bring more fish to the bank.

Lastly, there are books crafted by admirable wordsmiths, like Tom Fort and Chris Yates, which appeal to the more discerning reader and incurable romantic. The sort of angler who still hankers after the halcyon days when they fished overgrown, secret lakes and rivers using traditional split cane rods and centre pins.

I wish I were articulate enough to ruminate interminably about the philosophy of angling or wax lyrical about coaxing huge carp from the legendary Redmire Pool. Having never been lucky enough to fish there obviously I would not dare offer advice on the techniques one might use to catch such fish. And I certainly cannot chart my path to match-winning glory.

So this book does not fit neatly into conventional angling genre. You will, I'm afraid, not learn much about catching fish within these pages. Hopefully though, it might just provide a humorous insight into the psyche of a hapless angler and strike a chord with anyone who has ever fished for fun as a child and grown with the sport into adulthood.

Among Britain's three million strong angling fraternity, there are plenty out there, like me, who have never won a match in their lives, nor beamed out of the pages of *Angling Times* cradling a massive carp or catfish.

This book is about the life, trials and tribulations

of one such ordinary angler, someone who has a track record of falling in, losing big fish, and generally getting in one hell of a tangle. I only wish angling was the imperfect science Sky TV *Tight Lines* presenter Keith Arthur reckons it is. I would have been bagging up for years.

If Isaac Walton was the 'Compleat Angler', then I suppose, I am by comparison the 'incomplete angler'. Unfortunately, some of my compatriots love nothing more than to confer a supercilious title upon themselves. "I'm a professional matchman pal, I never pleasure fish." Or "I'm a specialist, mate. I'm only interested in catching specimen barbel or carp over thirty pounds." Tackle manufacturers have compounded these divisions within the family of angling, by targeting their products at specific groups using brand names like the 'matchmen' or 'specialist' range.

But the vast body of British anglers – the silent majority – fish as a form of relaxation, a therapy to the stresses and strains of modern life. They still compete against the fish, and the environment in which they live, not against the other anglers around them. Even the majority of those, like myself, who fish at club level, do so for the pleasure of it and because they rejoice in the sense of camaraderie as much as the competition.

Irritatingly, some of those who crave the notoriety of winning matches or chasing records, have moulded the description 'pleasure angler' into a derogatory term suggesting anyone who doesn't share their values, or dedication, is a 'Noddy angler' or 'deckchair'. What sanctimonious drivel. While I cannot remember the last time I fished from a deckchair, it is a truism that it doesn't matter to fish how much the seat-box or chair, you sit on, cost.

The fact that I have no match wins under my belt, or record-breaking specimens to my credit, does not mean I am any less devoted to, or passionate about, my sport, nor concerned about its future. Indeed, I have strong views on certain issues.

Though it hasn't always been so frequent, these days, I fish at least once a week throughout the year, and more often during the summer months. Sometimes I catch, and catch well, other times I don't, and go home slightly deflated, though never discouraged or disheartened. However, if the company is agreeable or the surroundings particularly beautiful, catching becomes academic anyway.

At the age of 53, I have recognised how important fishing is to my mental well-being, and appreciate its invigorating properties on my humdrum life. In my eyes, it is almost a spiritual experience, a connection with nature. The sense of anticipation alone is enough to set my adrenaline pumping.

Maria, my long-suffering wife, has been known to shake her head in disbelief when she sees me concocting a new paste, flavouring pellets in the garage, or building delicate pole rigs in my study, until I tell her such preparation rituals are an integral part of the enjoyment and satisfaction. I only wish I were better at it after all these years. Believe me, I have tried. I've read the manuals, watched the videos, and even sat behind and watched some famous, and naturally gifted, anglers. But whatever guile or innate skill they possess I have been unable to find it in my locker. Thus if you are, like me, perpetually unlucky and unceasingly accident prone, you eventually come to terms with your limitations and learn to enjoy whether you catch or not.

While I still dream of one day landing a 2lb roach

and carp of at least 20lbs, I somehow doubt a qualifying sample of either species will ever grace my net.

If I am honest, my biggest problem has always been an inability to cast, and feed, accurately. Even when clipped up I can still find an overhanging branch on an island at 30 yards range.

While I have learned to appreciate the joys of fishing with my coveted Mark IV split cane rod and Aerial centre pin, the pole has revolutionised my fishing during the past decade. These carbon wands have saved the day for me and enabled me to reach the same fish holding spots as anglers far more skilful than I, using rod and line. I suspect that is true for many. Poles have afforded me a degree of control, feeding accuracy and presentation I could only dream of when my great angling journey started back in 1963.

After spending the best part of the last 25 years writing about football at all levels, I believe the time is finally right to put pen to paper about the other sporting love of my life. But as you will hopefully read in the forthcoming pages, my quest for piscatorial perfection has been fraught with more than my share of angling disasters, scrapes and comic capers, some of which, it should be said, might be regarded as peripheral to actually catching fish!

Having bowed to pressure from friends to share those experiences, I hope this book evokes memories of all those days when you laughed out loud at someone else's antics or misfortune, or they laughed at yours. If it brings a smile to your face as a consequence, it will have achieved it's simple objective.

Peter Bishop 2004

Chapter 1
Cane and not so able...

As the fluorescent green No 16 elastic threaded through the top sections of my trusty pole did it's job and subdued another eight pounds of commercial fishery carp, I reflected on how such tackle, and venues, might have transformed my early experiences of fishing, and led to a lot less tangles and a good deal more fish in the net...

If angling legend John Wilson was virtually born with a rod in his hands, my own interest in the noble art was somewhat latent and entirely the result of sharing a bench during chemistry with a thin, sallow-faced boy of Irish extraction, by the name of Ian Courtney.

Indeed, for the first eleven years of my life I had been blissfully unaware of such piscatorial joys preferring to pursue interests as diverse as spotting fire engines, searching quarries for fossils, and collecting bird's eggs.

Though I had watched my Uncle Sidney fly fish for trout on small burns in Scotland, coarse fishing was entirely alien to me and had never crossed my mind.

Unlike many boys of that age who enjoyed the encouragement of a sport-playing father, mine admitted to only a passing interest in rugby and no knowledge whatsoever of fishing.

Thus the transformation effected by young Courtney was nothing short of genuine metamorphosis, and must have mortified my doting parents.

Instead of following my father in the pursuit of excellence in physics and chemistry, thoughts of owning a Richard Walker Mark IV split cane rod or catching a tench from a pond not far away from our home occupied most of my waking hours.

Now, don't get the idea I am in any way blaming Ian for distracting me from my studies. I desperately *wanted* to be sidetracked from positive and negative magnetic fields, chlorides and oxidisation. My father may have found such subjects engrossing but I certainly didn't.

But schoolboys are nothing if not ingenious when it comes to finding ways of making learning that bit more enjoyable. It really is amazing what you can achieve with the scientific application of a Bunsen burner, glass of water, gas pipe and half-pint of white maggots.

Among the discoveries made by the 'little and large' duo of Courtney and Bishop was the startling fact that during races down the inkwell, a maggot moved faster when subjected to a shot of town gas; maggots shrivel when boiled in water, and casters made a real mess of litmus paper when heated over a Bunsen burner.

Inseparable schoolmates and fishing partners, Ian and I extended our learning curve in geography by mapping ponds and lakes, averaged and calculated fish weights in maths and drew illustrations of float and tackle boxes in technical drawing.

Not surprisingly, my school reports reflected my aversion to academia and infuriating preference for "daydreaming about fishing".

It is a sad and regrettable fact that most 12-year-olds today are more likely to be interested in skateboards and playing 'Mortal Combat' on Playstations, than fishing.

Even worse, some have discovered fashion and girls,

and spend their weekends traipsing around shops looking for designer 'trainers' and tops while the less well-heeled hang around street corners whinging "I'm bored".

But back in 1963, when the Beatles released *Please, Please Me*, there were more than twenty confirmed anglers in our year, and the year below, and we knew of several senior boys who fished, because we saw them in John Parkes' fishing shop next door to the school.

I have often wondered if mere coincidence led Mr J. A. Parkes to site his angling emporium only fifty yards from a boys' secondary school.

Sandwiched between a tobacconists and a chip shop, the entire block of shops provided a heady cocktail of aromas to entice passing boys.

Those that skipped the delights of school dinners of brawn, mashed potato, and stewed cabbage, washed down by semolina pudding, often spent their dinner money, all five shillings of it, in one of those three establishments.

Some opted for ten Park Drive cigarettes if they could get a fifth year to purchase them on their behalf, while others settled for a 'healthy' fishcake and chips daily diet costing ninepence a day.

Ian and I quickly figured out we could eat for three shillings a week and have enough change to buy a float, or some lead weights and hooks; even putting a little by towards that much-coveted Efgecco tackle box priced at twelve shillings and eleven pence. It seemed every day Ian and I – with several other disciples in tow – would spend our dinner hour gazing wistfully at the vast array of quill floats, line, reels and rods that filled the glass cabinets around the shop floor, totally entranced by the combined fragrance of aniseed maggots, strawberry-flavoured groundbait, rubber gumboots and leather holdalls.

With enduring patience, the owner, John Parkes, allowed us to handle the rods and reels, put up the umbrellas, and even sift our grubby hands through the bins of bread crumb. No doubt he was confident that such encouragement would eventually bear fruit when we had sufficient saved, or managed to persuade our parents to accompany us at birthday or Christmas times.

A tall, gaunt man with a flock of swept back grey hair, who implausibly also played in a band, Johnny Parkes was our principal source of that commodity so rare then, but so abundant today: information.

Not withstanding *Mr Crabtree Goes Fishing* and the articles which appeared in *Angling Times*, it was the ever genial and avuncular Johnny Parkes who told us where to fish, what sort of tactics were required, and sold us the necessary licences. He even drew maps of the river and canal, marking good swims with an X. You don't get customer care like that from mail order tackle companies.

If Parksy inspired us to eventually venture beyond our local ponds, it was Ian who did the real groundwork teaching me the basics, like how to tie a hook, shot a float and cast. Apart from the admirable ability to fart loudly, almost at will, Ian also possessed a natural flair for fishing, so I was not surprised he developed into an accomplished match angler on the north west circuit. Simply by watching him, I learned where to find fish in a swim, how to hook a maggot correctly, how to mix groundbait, and most importantly, remove hooks with a disgorger so there was no damage to the fish's mouth. If only he had been able to show me how to unpick tangled nylon…

As far as I can recall my first ever fishing trip was a clandestine affair without the knowledge of my parents.

An overnight stay at Ian's house proved a useful cover for an early morning excursion to a farmer's pond, affectionately known to all the youngsters locally as the 'Polo', about a mile from Ian's house.

It must have been around 5.00am when we quietly slipped out and rode bikes down the deserted lane alongside fields shrouded in early morning mist.

Set in the middle of a lush green field, the 'Polo' was hidden from view by a cluster of mighty oaks and elms, standing like mourners huddled at a graveside. At one end a weeping willow bowed to kiss the water's edge.

Having negotiated the gate to the lane and pushed our bikes through the dew laden grass, the hazy sunlight highlighted the only clear path through the undergrowth to reveal a reed fringed, heart-shaped pond, no more than a third of an acre in size. Largely choked by water lilies, there was sufficient space for maybe six or seven people to fish without getting in each other's way.

An idyllic setting, except for the rusting remains of an old motorbike partly submerged amongst the lilies! Apparently, no club rented the water and the farmer allowed boys, and the occasional adult, to fish it; but there was a hand-painted sign asking visitors to take home their rubbish – obviously excluding motorcycles – and close the gate after them.

According to Ian, the pond contained roach, rudd, perch, crucian carp and tench. There were also rumours of a big mirror carp. Some fifth year boys in Johnny Parkes claimed to have heard a crash and witnessed the bow wave as it radiated out from some point in the middle of the lilies. No one though had ever caught it. Given schoolboys are inclined to exaggerate, the carp was reputed to be at least 20lbs!

In those days big carp – and in truth a pond of that size would probably not have been able to sustain anything larger than 6lbs – were regarded as virtually uncatchable. In 1963 few anglers bothered with them – with the notable exception of Dick Walker who famously captured 'Clarissa' at a record 44lbs from Redmire Pool ten seasons earlier. We knew all about, and indeed were in awe of, 'Clarissa' because John Parkes had a framed black and white picture, personally autographed by Dick Walker, on his shop counter.

Today, the angling press is full of pictures of 13-year-olds proudly showing off carp in excess of 25lbs; something which is indicative of the revolution which has taken place in both tackle and tactics during the intervening period. Certainly, Ian's fishing tackle would not have landed the carp in the 'Polo' never mind 'Clarissa', but that didn't deter schoolboys from dreaming that one day they might slide the net under a such a monster.

I watched transfixed as Ian assembled his whole cane rod with split cane tip, attached a Intrepid fixed spool reel carrying 3lbs BS line, and then competed the terminal tackle with a favourite peacock quill float supporting a tiny size 18 hook baited with two white maggots.

With a gentle underarm cast he dropped the float as close as possible to the lilies, threw a handful of maggots around it, placed the rod in the rest, and sat down to wait.

It can only have been five minutes before the red tip bobbled twice before disappearing beneath the surface and after a brief resistance a small golden fish the size of my hand disturbed the early morning silence by splashing around on the surface. Ian lifted a small crucian carp clean out the water and into his waiting hand.

Then came those immortal words that would come

back to haunt me for years, "See, it's easy once you know what to do."

Four more crucians, a perch and a rudd followed before it was my turn to sit on Ian' wicker basket. My heart pounded with a mixture of excitement and trepidation, as I prepared to cast a line for the first time. All I had to do was copy what Ian did.

After my initial attempt at an underarm swing fell well short of the lilies, Ian told me to open the bale arm, put my finger on the line and cast over my head, releasing the line when the rod passed 10 o'clock, just as we had practised in his garden.

But overhanging branches from large oak trees did not surround Ian's garden. Adopting an entirely unexpected trajectory, the float, shot and baited hook soared upwards and wound themselves in perfect symmetry around the largest and most densely foliaged branch. My very first tangle – and sadly not the last!

Unfazed by my incompetence poor Ian had to pull for a break before setting up the terminal tackle all over again.

This time, Ian cast the line before passing the rod to me and sure enough a few minutes later one of the most significant moments in the life of Peter Bishop occurred. As the quill float slipped away, a deft sweep of the rod, which would have ripped the teeth out of a great white shark's mouth, ensured a four-inch long roach hurtled past my right ear at a rate of knots. "You don't have to strike *that* hard," chided Ian as I picked the flapping fish up from the hardened mud bank.

But it wasn't just the roach that was hooked, it was me. At last, I had found a sport in which I could compete on an equal footing to those of my peer group who were physically lighter and more agile – or so I thought.

Though I didn't tell them where and when I had enjoyed this momentous experience, I told my parents I had been fishing using someone else's gear and enjoyed it so much I now wanted to buy my own rod and reel so I could go with my friends regularly.

Though an only child – my mother didn't have me until she was 38 – my parents nevertheless decided they would resist the temptation to over-indulge me. While we were, I suppose, 'comfortable', due to my father's job as a scientist for the Atomic Energy Authority, fishing rods and reels were still the sort of items that constituted birthday or Christmas presents.

Despite my father's reservations because I couldn't swim (and still can't) he agreed to bring forward my birthday by two months, and one Saturday morning we headed off to Johnny Parkes' haven of fishing tackle.

Though I had only been fishing a couple of times, I was nevertheless clear in my own mind about what sort of gear would be not only appropriate, but would earn me some 'street cred', as they now call it, from other anglers on the bank.

After all, no self-respecting fisherman would want to be seen with one of those pathetic 7ft fibreglass rods from Woolworths!

Despite all the persuasive arguments put to him regarding the benefits of investing in a Richard Walker Mark IV Avon split cane rod and a 'Allcocks Aerial' centre pin reel (it would be almost 40 years before I finally bought both as collectors' items), I had to settle for a much cheaper 11ft Forshaws 'Palace B' whole cane rod with a fibreglass tip costing £3 10. 0d and a Daiwa fixed spool reel costing £2. 5. 0d.

Now, you may wonder quite how I can be so precise about this now. Well, ever since those early days I have kept fishing diaries and all my fishing equipment and how much it cost, was itemised within its pages. Though somewhat tattered now, they are still legible and record the date, venue, weather conditions, fish caught, bait and tackle used, who went and other items of note. They have since proved an invaluable source of information and memory prompter.

Apart from line, some floats, lead shot and a selection of hooks, like Ronnie Barkers' famous shop owner character, 'Arkwright', Johnny Parkes managed to convince my father of the necessity of a landing net, small keep net and a wicker basket to sit on. By the time we departed, he had been 'fleeced' to the tune of over £12 – a considerable amount of money at the time.

"I hope this isn't going to be one of your passing fads," groaned my father as we climbed into his aqua marine coloured Austin Cambridge loaded down with tackle.

Well it wasn't, and 40 years on I am still in love with angling despite the fact my casting is still not much better than it was that June morning at the 'Polo'!

Chapter 2
In at the deep end

Throughout the summer of 1964 I continued to cut my angling teeth on the 'Polo' but widened my search for good fishing to two other nearby ponds. One was known as the 'Sytch' while the other was called the 'Rec', ostensibly because it was sited in the middle of a council owned playing field. In reality, the Rec was mainly used for what dog owners euphemistically call 'exercising their animals', which made crossing this patch of grassland an act of faith.

The pond itself was almost circular and had a couple of old oak trees at one end while the other was merely fringed with reeds and a tree stump.

The 'Rec' was full of small roach and crucians, which responded well to a diet of maggots, steamed bread and hemp seed. Though the fish were small in size it was nevertheless possible to amass quite a bag of fish using light tackle.

If there was a problem with the Rec it was that the playing field was regularly frequented by older youths on drinking binges.

Given my parents imposed a 9.00pm curfew, the only way I could get around it and fish on into the evening was to lie and say I was staying at Ian's house. On this particular evening he had told his father that *he* was sleeping at my house, but had in fact surreptitiously removed a large green tent from his shed before his father came home. On the basis there was strength in numbers, two other friends from school, Philly Prichard and George Taylor – who was in the year above us – were invited to join us and we all squeezed into the one tent which was erected beneath the mutilated oak tree which guarded the Recs' pond.

To spice up the evening's proceedings, Philly had liberated a large bottle of Sherry from his dad's booze cupboard. For my part, I had managed to 'borrow' some cigarettes from my mother's opened packet of 20. Oh, how grown up we felt smoking and drinking in the tent. With a bottle to share and plenty of dirty jokes to relate, we elected not to fish too late that evening but awake at first light and grab the best swims before anyone else turned up.

Our tackle safe inside the tent the question of vulnerability to attack never occurred to our naive and alcohol stupefied minds.

Unfortunately, we hadn't bargained for a gang of 16 year-olds who, having consumed copious amounts of illicit beer, spotted our tent beneath the trees by the Pond and decided to terrorise the occupants.

In our own alcoholic haze the first sign of danger was the sound of slurred voices outside the tent. Ian recognised one. It was 'Creaker', an obnoxious fifth year with a reputation as a bit of a hard case. There were plenty like him at our school. Tough? It was the only school in the borough with its own mortuary!

"Youzegorany ale in dere?" enquired another gruff voice. "No," we shouted squeakily, holding on tightly to the zip and ties that separated us from our attackers. It's amazing how fear sobers you up quickly.

"Dey wown 'ave any, dey're jus kids, probably playin' with demselves," snorted Creaker to his mates.

Almost instantaneously, the roof seemed to cave in

as the sides, tent pole and Tilly lamp all came crashing down around our heads. Someone outside had released, or cut, the guy ropes.

Like skydivers trapped in their parachutes, we rolled around in the green canvas and cotton as boots rained in on us. Philly took a kick in the plums, I got caught on the back of the head, but the effects of the cheap sherry dulled the pain. However, the thing that hurt most was sound of splintered cane as I rolled over and crushed my own rod in its cotton bag.

After a volley of expletives, all went quiet as the gang, as they usually do, ran off across the field whooping and laughing leaving us to unravel ourselves and extinguish the simmering Tilly lamp by the only method available – pee on it. Well, you couldn't pour sherry on it, could you?

In the moonlight we pulled ourselves together and assessed the damage. Apart from a large scorch mark in the tent, George's landing net pole was bent, the contents of Ian's basket was all over the place and worst of all there was a long split in the middle section of my Forshaws cane rod and two rings were flattened. The fact that I had a bruise to the back of head the size of a boiled egg was immaterial.

Now the wimpy thing to do would have been to run off home, but we were made of sterner stuff. It was a clear warm August night so we simply slept under the stars cradling our tackle – fishing tackle that is – just in case anyone else attempted to separate us from it. Around 5.00am we awoke and started fishing. Given the split in my rod George loaned me his spare and by 8.00am my keepnet contained several roach and perch plus a superb specimen crucian that must have been 8–10oz. Now, you might scoff at that these days but in my eyes a fish of that size deserved special mention in my fishing diary.

Of course, my parents knew nothing of the camping expedition so I explained the damage to my rod was the result of accidentally standing on it when packing up. Expecting to have to fork out for a new middle section, I was indebted to Johnny Parkes once again when he saved the day with two new rings and a superb whipping to cover the split which was probably stronger than the original cane beneath.

The strength of the rod was given a severe test a few weeks later, but not by a fish. During a typical British summer we were rained off one morning and retreated to Ian's house to dry out. A few hours later and the sun was again cracking the flags and Ian was getting itchy feet. First, we decided to practice ground baiting by bowling a tennis ball underarm into a bucket positioned ten yards down the garden. It was a sign of things to come that Ian managed to drop the ball into the bucket nine times out of ten, whilst I succeeded just twice! One of my 'efforts' even cracked the glass window of the garden shed five yards further down the garden.

Sensing my inaccuracy might lead to further damage and earache from his long-suffering father, Ian suggested a more harmless test. Who could cast a piece of bread crust the furthest? All was going reasonably well until a huge seagull suddenly swooped into the garden, grabbed the bread off the lawn and took off leaving me fighting a frantic aerial battle.

As the tethered bird twisted and turned in mid air drawing yards off my reel, my rod bent into a parabolic curve testing Johnny Parkes' repair to the limit. As I was never going to land the bird I decided there was only one thing to do and cut the line. But before Ian could find any scissors the line snapped and my biggest catch so far flew off. For months I was unmercifully ribbed about the incident, "That will be the only bird you ever pull," said Ian. He wasn't far wrong!

The arrival of my fourteenth birthday, brought an unexpected bonus to my tackle collection as unbeknown to me my father had been dispatched to Johnny Parkes with instructions from aunt Muriel (my mother's spinster sister) to "get him an umbrella so the pour soul doesn't get drenched".

There was also a rod holdall from my gran. "So you won't break the rod if you stand on it again you clumsy bugger," sneered my father. If only he knew the truth...

Over the coming winter months both saw sterling service as Ian and I ventured further afield than the 'Polo'. It's not as if our favourite venue was no longer up to it. There was great fun to be had there during the summer holidays, and during one early morning session, Ian somehow managed to bully a good tench from the sanctuary of the lilly pads using his new Apollo Taperflash tubular steel rod.

It was just that some of the older boys at school had relayed tales of catching big bream from the Shropshire Union canal near Backford and net full's of roach by the suspension bridge on the River Dee in Chester. Johnny Parkes, no doubt with an eye to maggot sales, was also keen for us to experience the joys of trotting running water and told us of the best swims to fish and techniques to use. Of course, one would never admit to the older lads that we hadn't *actually* fished these venues, as our parents would not let us travel that far unaccompanied.

It was best to nod in agreement and say something like, "Well, I had ten pounds last week off the bandstand swim on the Groves."

Given my parents showed no inclination to allow me to venture further afield to sample the delights of the canal and river, I persuaded my father to drive us there, drop us off by the canal while they went shopping and then pick us up later.

Johnny Parkes, as usual, was happy to supply a canal licence – excellent value at five shillings (25p) for a whole season – plus advice on where to fish. Some hot pegs at the back of the Bowling Alley and a bay next to the City Walls were said to produce good-sized bream and roach.

Armed with a pint of maggots, some red groundbait laced with hemp, and a lump of steamed bread, all our gear was loaded into the back my father's Austin Cambridge. My parents dropped us off near the canal, arranged a pick up time, and headed off shopping for the day.

After studying Johnny Parkes' sketch we decided to fish from a narrow concrete bank bounded by a wooden fence which separated the towpath from a lane which ran down the back of the Bowling Alley. Within half an hour of our arrival, three other friends from school, Tommy Bywater, Steve Gurnell and his elder brother Mike turned up having travelled the 12 miles from home by Crosville bus. Not surprisingly, they chose to join us on the narrow towpath by the fence.

Canal fishing posed several problems that we hadn't encountered before on still water ponds. For a start there was a gentle flow which was accentuated every time the locks on the next stretch were opened, and there were boats.

Johnny Parkes said the bream tended to be nomadic but often liked to shoal up in the bays, but that there were plenty of roach and perch to be found by the marginal shelves and in a deeper channel down the middle.

Given Ian always seemed to know instinctively what to do I copied his set up and fixed a quill float top and bottom with most of my shot near the hook length.

Using my plummet I established it was about five feet deep down the middle and three foot right in front of me. It was information that would come in handy later.

Taking Ian's advice I mixed my groundbait quite dry so it was stiff, cast out, and put the rod in its rest. Taking careful aim with the first ball I bowled underarm. The ball hit the water a good four feet from my float, the second was a foot short and the third broke up into little pieces mid air and scattered into the water.

The accuracy of my ground baiting had not improved from that afternoon in Ian's garden.

Mind you, I didn't matter minutes later. To our horror the flow suddenly accelerated and it was all I could do to hold back my float as it bobbled around uncontrollably. It was as if someone had let the plug out of a bath. Great clouds of mud coloured the water as the bottom silt was disturbed. Ten minutes later 'Captain Pugwash' appeared, resplendent in striped jersey and peaked cap, at the helm of a thirty-foot long houseboat.

As the craft chugged by creating a bow wave which lapped over our feet, someone shouted, "Ahoy me hearties, is 'Seaman Staines' and 'Master Bates' aboard?" before all five of us fell into fits of juvenile laughter.

In those days, the sexual innuendo contained in a children's TV cartoon might have been too subtle for BBC Executives, but it certainly wasn't lost on teenage schoolboys. Captain Pugwash glared at us. Using his bait throwing stick Tommy flicked some maggots in his general direction.

Despite the nuisance of the boat traffic, Ian and Mike Gurnell had caught some small roach on white maggot, but the rest of us were facing the 'blank' – something I have got used to over the years! This canal fishing, I thought, is not all it is cracked up to be. It must have been around 1.30pm when I stood up to lift the lid of my basket and extract the sandwiches my mother had lovingly prepared from the jumble of hook packets, shot containers, tins and other junk.

Anyone who has sat in one position for some length of time knows you can sometimes suffer slight dizziness when you first stand up. That fraction of a second was enough for me to lose my balance momentarily.

Time stood still, as if I was falling in slow motion, as I realised what was about to happen and frantically grabbed at fresh air in a desperate attempt to defy the laws of gravity and readjust my balance. It was fruitless. With a mighty splash, befitting a tall and portly teenager already nearly 5ft 9in tall, I hit the cold water and sank into the dark abyss.

As the bank disappeared from view and all went silent, water filled my nose, ears and eyes bringing about a feeling of sheer panic, as the prospect of drowning visited my subconscious. Thanks to the buoyancy affect of air trapped in my anorak, and the fact my wellington boots seemed to find something firm, if not clingy to rest upon, I flapped around like a large waterfowl and managed to right myself so my head broke the surface. Spitting canal water from my mouth and wiping my eyes I saw Ian crouched and offering me a landing net handle to grab onto.

Though I didn't see my predicament as worthy of

laughter it seemed as if everyone else found it hilarious! Holding onto the net pole as if it were a life belt I tried to ease myself up the nearside shelf in an effort to gain a footing and climb out.

But the weight of water in my wellies made that prohibitive, and for a few moments I swirled around bringing up huge clouds of sediment off the bottom before being half hauled from the water by the combined efforts of Ian, Tommy, Mike and Steve.

It was at that juncture a passing man on a bike delivered the coup de grace and sent everyone back into peels of laughter at my expense.

"Jesus!" exclaimed the man, "I never knew they grew to that fucking size in this canal. What did it take? Maggots?" and pedalled off chortling to himself no doubt delighted by his witticism.

As 'luck' would have it my father, having parked not too far away, decided to return to the car early and shed some of the load of shopping bags he had been carrying and decided to look in on us en route. I must have made a pathetic sight huddled on the bankside, shivering and barefoot having emptied the wellies.

When my father's anger subsided, and the crowd who had gathered to share in my discomfort dispersed, I was helped back to the car with all my gear. "I said this would happen," he groaned predictably.

"What about a lift for Ian?" I suggested tentatively. "He can get the bus home with those lads," growled my father. "He'll need some new buddies because you won't be going fishing again until you can swim!"

Chapter 3
Pain in the backside

It was some weeks before the hullabaloo over falling in the canal subsided. My father was at pains to point out I could have drowned, while I argued I was with swimmers and the water wasn't that deep.

Of course it is eminently sensible for every angler to be able to swim but I have always argued that as long as you take reasonable precautions and know the depth of water in front of you, fishing can be as safe as any other pastime. True, I have fallen in since on a number of occasions, but they are stories for another time...

I have tried to learn to swim on a number of occasions – the last being when my own children learned – but have never quite cracked it and at 53, it seems pointless to try now. If I know water is likely to be deep I wear my Fox inflatable life jacket.

Somehow, I have never managed to conquer the trauma I suffered as a result of being pushed into the deep end of a swimming pool by a group of older boys when I was just six years old. Without my father's intervention I would have undoubtedly drowned.

While my back flip into the canal granted me celebrity status at school as the butt of many a joke, I couldn't tell my schoolmates my father had locked my fishing tackle in the shed until "you come to your senses". But I was adamant that I would not give up fishing. It was a case of the immovable object versus the irresistible force.

Eventually, he did relent but there had obviously been much debate between my parents. As often happened, my mother brokered a peace deal that involved him taking me fishing by car, so he could keep an eye on me. For my part, I had to agree to swimming lessons again and also teach my father to fish.

Having largely outgrown ponds like the 'Polo' and the 'Rec', I could see definite advantages to this arrangement. There was only one problem, my father had no tackle. Uncle Sidney produced a 9ft split cane fly rod and reel but I explained this would not do the job. Clearly, the only solution to this deficiency was another pilgrimage to Johnny Parkes piscatorial paradise. Though Ian had a fancy for a Milbro Enterprise I had had my eye on an Abu Mark 5 13ft hollow fibreglass match rod for some time – and had examined it in detail – but at £13 odd, my chances of owning one was, I believed, fairly slim.

However, my father's impending introduction to the world of angling put a different complexion on the situation. A degree of subterfuge was required to turn any expenditure to my advantage. I reasoned that if Johnny Parkes could persuade my father to buy the Abu I could lay claim to it and he could inherit the patched up Forshaws cane rod. Better still, Parksy would offer a reduced price for two Abu rods. I asked him to suggest it.

My cunning plan worked a treat. Like 'Arkright', Johnny Parkes made the purchase of two Abu Mark 5 match rods and an Abu 505 closed face reel seem such a bargain my father caved in and left the shop some £28 lighter than he went in!

Over the next few weeks father took Ian and I fishing a couple of times and we in turn showed him how to tie a hook, shot and fix a float and cast. As he did with most things, he mastered everything very quickly, and was soon casting – using my old Daiwa reel – with greater accuracy than I did.

The availability of transport opened up all sorts of new horizons for Ian – whose father didn't drive – and I. One venue we had heard about but never visited was a flooded quarry in Waverton, about 16 miles from home. According to Johnny Parkes – who else – it was open to anyone to fish and was stuffed with big tench and carp but there were only a few fishable swims. Given recent history and the depth of water my father was understandably cautious but we nevertheless decided to give it a go.

The quarry was indeed deep and mysterious, almost 40ft in places, but quite sheltered due to being in a hollow surrounded by ash and birch trees. Steep cliffs surrounded most of the lake but at one end there was a long ramp leading down to a plateau by the water's edge.

My father parked in the lane and we climbed the gate and followed the path.

None of us had ever encountered a lake so deep. "My guess is the fish will be up in the water looking for food as it drops in," said Ian with an air of authority. Though it was difficult casting, I set the depth at almost 10ft and kept a regular trickle of maggots going in around my float.

Ian enjoyed first blood when a roach of nearly half a pound hungrily snapped up his double maggot offering on the drop. Soon after, my float slid under and the tip of my Abu Mark 5 bent around under the force of a very good fish. Making an angle against the running fish I cranked the 505 reel as Ian instructed, back winding the drag to give line when the fish plunged deeper. My heart raced as the breeze made the taunt line sing in falsetto. Just when I was beginning to think I'd never get control of it, a plump green tench, bigger than anything I had seen before, broke the surface and thrashed about, before Ian gingerly slipped the net under it.

I could not have been more euphoric if I had landed a British record and let out a huge whooping 'yeeesss' scream that echoed and reverberated around the quarry walls. "Steady on!" scolded my father. We duly weighed my prize catch which tipped the scales at 2lb 10ozs. Today, no one bats an eye lid at 4–5lb tench, but in the angling circles in which I moved then, a fish of any sort over a pound was a specimen to behold.

A few more roach and rudd around 8oz added to my sense of elation, and my father was particularly pleased with a pristine roach of 14ozs that took his bait a second or so after it hit the water. Up on the nearby road, bells and sirens from a passing police car or fire engine intruded upon the eerie peace.

Our contentment was suddenly interrupted though by the sound of a loudhailer booming around the walls of the quarry. "This is Cheshire Constabulary, is there anyone down there? Is everything OK?"

My father and I stared at each other in open-mouthed bemusement. Just then two policemen and three firemen, carrying ropes, marched down the ramp with walkie-talkies chattering away.

"Had someone fallen in, was a swimmer in difficulty?" they enquired. Apparently, the lady who lived in the cottage opposite the quarry had heard a blood-curdling scream, figured someone was drowning, and dialled 999.

My father claimed he had never felt so stupid in his

life explaining that the yelling was the result of teenage exuberance at catching a big tench!

Fortunately, the police found it mildly amusing, and accepted there was no malice on our part, however it was some time before we returned to the quarry.

My father had spotted a beautiful looking pond on a farm in Cuddington where he and my mother had stopped to buy eggs and asked the owner if we could fish. It turned out to be a little gem and became a venue my father, Ian and I would visit many times together.

Though the roach and rudd rarely exceeded 6oz in size, they were nevertheless plentiful and it was not usual to bag upwards of 70 fish in an afternoon session. My father even caught a tench of 1¼lbs.

While ponds were, and still are to this day, my first love, Ian was adamant that we needed to become proficient at catching on the canal if we were to aspire to 'match angling'.

According to the word of some matchmen in Johnny Parkes' shop, the most popular stretch of the canal for big matches was called the 'Golden Nook'.

After fishing the section with Ian a couple of times I felt sufficiently confident of catching to suggest we call in there one day whilst out on a family outing with my parents and my mother's spinster sister, Muriel.

Auntie Muriel was very much my father's cross to bear. In marrying my mother I don't think he had bargained for taking on her elder sister as well. When my grandparents on my mothers side died my aunt moved down to England after selling the family home in Aberdeen, and bought a house in the same avenue, not six doors away from my parents. Her customary presence in our house may explain why my father bought a Myford lathe and spent most of his time building model ships and planes in the shed. What made things worse was the fact she had no sense of humour and was often the butt of my father's jokes.

Whilst my father and I fished the Golden Nook, my mother and aunt sat on the towpath in folding deckchairs enjoying the September sunshine. While my mother was a compulsive knitter, aunt Muriel preferred reading romantic novels.

Having adopted the same heavy groundbaiting approach which had worked for Ian and I previously, and set up a 'stret pegging' arrangement on both my rod and my father's, we did well to liberate five good sized bream from the boat track before a precession of pleasure boats stirred up the bottom and killed the swim.

Glancing around I noticed that my aunt was no longer sitting behind us.

The howl that followed could even be heard above the chug-chug of the boat engines. "Kathleeeen!" My mother jumped up and moved sharply towards some bushes and undergrowth that separated the canal towpath from the road alongside.

"Oh Johnny," shouted my mother. "Muriel's fallen in some nettles, you've got to help her." My father and I wound in our lines and put the rods in their rests before following my mother into a little hollow. "You stay here Peter," said my mother anxious to protect her sister's modesty.

But I could see perfectly well what had happened. Attempting a call of nature, my aunt had gone into the bushes, hitched up her pleated skirt, and lowered her knickers, only to lose her balance as she crouched, and fall backwards into a huge clump of nettles. She was sobbing uncontrollably with the pain. Sensing that proof of the existence of God was right in front of him, my father first bit his lip, then doubled up in laughter, which only accentuated my aunts' anger and embarrassment.

"Go and get some dock leaves!" ordered my mother sharply. My father, still convulsed with laughter, picked up the smallest dock leaf he could find and handed it to his prostrate sister-in-law, who glared at him through gritted teeth.

Rubbing his hands together in a gesture of satisfaction as we returned to our pegs, my father turned to me and whispered, "Your auntie's arse looks just like the Japanese flag!"

While my mother dabbed dock leaves on the bright red posterior of her elder sister apologising for my father's warped sense of humour, we reluctantly packed up in the sure knowledge this fishing trip would end in the A&E department of Clatterbridge General Hospital.

Though I was grateful for the transport to these far away venues, at nearly fifteen I was nevertheless keen to throw off the shackles of the family and make my own way in the world. One day a solution presented itself when George Taylor announced he had been accepted as member of one of the local angling clubs who organised weekly coach trips to different venues around the area.

They also leased dozens of small farm ponds from the local estate landowners. Every week the coach picked up members and took them to the likes of the Golden Nook, the Dee and Buckley Flash, but the best venue of them all was the Manor lake itself.

This was a venue we were well aware of because we had, I am ashamed to say, poached it along with most other lads in the locality. Indeed, we had regularly played a game of cat and mouse with the gamekeepers, who patrolled the fringes of the lake armed with shot-guns loaded with rock salt.

Having crossed a field of wheat and scaled a sand-stone wall, we used to crawl through the undergrowth like army sappers to reach the edge of the lilly-covered lake. Twice we succeeded in catching a few crucians and tench before the barking of the gun dogs gave away the impending approach of the 'Gamey', thus allowing suf-ficient time to grab you gear and 'leg it' through the rho-dodendron bushes, over the wall, and across the field to our bikes.

On the third occasion, it seems the gamekeepers had outwitted us, and mounted a military pincer move-ment, using Landrovers, to cut off our retreat. Dressed in their plus fours and deerstalkers they were guarding our bikes near the lane.

Seeing us coming though the field they challenged us to stop, but there was no way we were hanging around to get caught. "Run for it," shouted someone. Being heavier, and therefore slower, than the others, I was bringing up the rear when I heard a gunshot, which was immediately followed by a stinging sensa-tion in my buttocks and lower back.

It brought me temporarily to a halt, dropping my old rod and bag. I cried out. Looking behind me I could see smoke billowing from the gun barrel. The gamekeeper yelled "Come here you little bastards," as he reloaded. Even though the stinging pain in my backside was in-tense I kept running until we reached the gate, vaulted over it and beat a hasty retreat along the main road.

It was about a three-mile walk home and by the time I made it darkness had fallen and my parents were about to mobilise a search party. Given the seat of my blue jeans was peppered with small and bloodied holes, and likewise my tee shirt, there was no other option than to come clean.

Though my father was livid with me, he was outraged by the use of a shotgun. Poaching is one thing, he said, shooting at you, is another matter entirely. Despite his diatribe about pressing charges for 'inflicting GBH' my mother managed to dissuade him from complaining to the police on the basis I could end up getting prosecuted for trespass! As for the bike we would just have to write it off.

That evening was spent lying face down on my bed with my mother plucking tiny fragments of rock salt from the cheeks of my backside with a pair of sterilised tweezers and a tube of Germaline. "How in Christ's name do you get yourself into these bloody scrapes?" lamented my father. "You really are becoming a pain in the arse!"

Given my predicament at that particular moment, for once I had to agree with him!

Chapter 4
To the Manor sworn...

Following in the footsteps of Georgie Taylor, Ian and I applied to join the same angling club based in Port Sunlight, the unique model village adjacent to our school. For many years membership had been restricted to employees of Lever Brothers, and their families. As the number of factory workers, and indeed those interested in fishing, dwindled, so the club opened its doors to non-employees.

Having completed our application forms we were interviewed individually in a smoke filled room by the full committee, a particularly harrowing experience for a 15-year-old, and eventually informed by letter of our acceptance as 'junior members'. Along with the club card and rule book came a map detailing all the waters available to us and a list of all the away-day trips and coach pick-up points.

With up to 49 anglers aboard – most of whom smoked – plus all the slime-soiled clothing, wet nets and rancid maggots, I always pitied whoever inherited the coach on the Monday morning. By the time we vacated it the smell could have stopped a charging rhino in its tracks.

Looking down the 'fixture list', which included trips to the Rivers Weaver, Dee and Severn, there were some visits to the canal at Backford and the Golden Nook, so at least we had some experience to draw on when it came to matches.

The highlight of the season though would be the two trips to Thornton Manor. It would be strange returning there 'legally' for a change, and I did wonder if the gamekeepers might recognise me (or at least my backside) should they be around.

According to some of the senior members, matches on the Manor occasionally produced weights approaching the magical ton, which was at the time, virtually unheard of. There were roach, rudd and crucians to 2lbs plus, big tench over 5lbs and enormous perch and pike. It would be surprising if such a man-made estate lake didn't hold big carp, but as nobody bothered with them in those days, we were not able to confirm their existence.

No matter, the Manor trip was the most over-subscribed and eagerly anticipated trip of the summer.

Having acquired another bike, albeit secondhand, from a dealer in town, I spent many a summers morning, loaded down with basket and holdall, pedalling the three miles from home to the club ponds, but in truth they rarely lived up to expectations.

Dotted around the Cheshire landscape, each cluster of small farm ponds were ingeniously named 'A group', 'B group', and so on. Many though were choked with lilies and weed, and were largely unfishable, but we did catch plenty of small tench and crucians from one known as the 'roadside pond'.

Georgie Taylor, ever the clown, was often on hand to provide the entertainment doing some indescribable things with a tench which, while it didn't hurt the fish, sent everyone into raptures.

For my part, days of delight were mixed with days of despair when nothing seemed to go right. In trying to master a cheap Trudex centre pin reel I had purchased impulsively from a fifth former at school, no sooner had I set up the float, shot and hook than I often had to start all over again when the line ended up in a complete 'bird's nest' around the drum – in other words, another bloody tangle!

A number of huge overhanging oak tree branches didn't help either, but I soldiered on even though my patience was sorely tested to the limit on occasions.

The away-day trips by coach proved far more satisfying though we were left to fend for ourselves by most of the senior members in the club. They didn't want to know about juniors, an attitude, I gather, which was not uncommon in those days, as other anglers have since relayed similar experiences.

Today we have a much more enlightened approach to helping the next generation of anglers and most clubs, including my current one, have a vibrant junior section coached by senior members. As I have grown older, and a little wiser, I have always made a point of trying to help youngsters whenever I can, particularly if they appear to be struggling. Five minutes spent re-adjusting a rig, tying on a smaller hook or supplying a different bait can have a dramatic effect on a youngster's fishing success. Watching them catch thereafter is almost as satisfying as doing so yourself.

When we travelled to venues like the River Weaver at Hartford and the canal at Golden Nook, we found that vastly experienced anglers like Jack Egan, Jack Theobold and Jimmy Peers, who were regarded as the best in the club at that time, were not very forthcoming about their winning methods and baits.

I remember once asking Jimmy Peers what method and bait he had used to win a match on the Golden Nook. "Can you keep a secret son?" he asked. "Of course," I whispered, eagerly anticipating being shown his successful set up. "Well, so can I," snapped Jimmy, and that was the end of it! I can only imagine the senior members saw the young bucks as a challenge to their supremacy, and decided to put us in our place. Pathetic really.

The only person to offer Ian, George, Tommy and I any help, and informal coaching, was a member in his mid-twenties called Peter Cooke, who was to later open his own tackle shop in town. He, and his elder brother Eric, became our mentors, and there is no doubt Ian, in particular, owes much of his success as a match angler in later life to the techniques and tricks Peter showed us.

The first trip to the Manor was scheduled for late June and we all duly assembled at the rear entrance to the estate – that used by the staff and tradesmen – before trooping in under the watchful eyes of the game-keepers. Like a fugitive, I kept my sun-visor down just in case I was recognised.

In the glistening morning sunshine, the lake looked magnificent, and was far bigger than I had appreciated whilst confined to the top corner, poaching. Surrounded on three sides by mature oak, ash and alder trees, the lake was approximately six acres in size with several wooded islands dotted around one half, with a long narrow arm, covered in lilies, leading to a rectangular swimming pool at the other end.

A wide, expansive lawn at one end afforded an unobstructed view of the palatial sandstone manor house and ornamental garden, occupying an elevated position, maybe 300 yards away.

With the exception of some deep water in front of the old boathouse, the average depth was around 5ft but the canal arm was much shallower at 3ft. It was the archetypal English estate lake, dug out in the latter part of the 19th century by those who laid out the 60 acre estate and lush classical gardens.

The best peg reputedly was next to the sluice, but I drew peg 21 halfway up the canal arm amid several overhanging trees.

With large clumps of water lilies to the left, right, and in front of me it was certainly a swim that would test my casting skills. If ever a swim was made for tangles this was it, but the good thing was I could see at least three separate muddy clouds with pinhead bubbles. It was solid with feeding tench.

Beforehand, the ever-helpful Peter Cooke suggested I use the lift method with steamed bread on the hook for the tench, and maggots for the crucians. As always, it turned out to be sound advice.

Despite the tree branches and lily pads, much to my surprise I excelled myself and managed to bully and cajole several 'tincas' to 1½lbs from the swim before the action inevitably tailed off – miraculously without the loss of a single float or hook.

Even a heavy shower could not dampen my enthusiasm. Switching from the lift method to a small peacock quill and double maggot I was immediately into roach, rudd and perch up to half a pound, plus the odd small crucian, and by the halfway stage I felt I had maybe 15 pounds of fish in my net – much more than those around me.

Word on the bank was that Norman Lonsdale was caning them on the main lake but that I was in with a good chance of 'framing', as match anglers like to call it when you finish second, third or fourth.

Though I have never considered myself either

sufficiently competent, or competitive, to be a 'match angler', on this particular day the prospect of earning some brownie points, not just with my peers, but amongst those senior members who had snubbed me fired my determination. I wanted to prove a point.

Having followed Peter Cooke's advice of targeting the tench early and late, I switched back to the lift method and steamed bread with an hour to go and was immediately rewarded with three smallish tench.

Believing, somewhat naively, that I was actually on course for a placing, I concentrated almost obsessively on the hypnotic red tip of my balsa float, willing it to disappear. I was a study in determination.

With about ten minutes to go the tip of the float rose high and then lay flat on the surface, as if it had somehow become detached from the lead weight that cocked it.

Without waiting for a further invitation, I swept the rod to my right and connected with a solid lump, definitely a big fish, which seemed so stunned by the pressure I was exerting it decided to surface and see who, or what, was giving it grief.

The second I saw its vast green belly, possibly swelled with spawn, my jaw dropped. It was massive; maybe twice the size of the Waverton Quarry tench. This could be a match winner I concluded.

With a mighty sweep of her tail rudder, the big female plunged beneath the surface and headed for the sanctuary of the dense lily pads. Anticipating the worst, I screwed down the drag and held on for dear life. My trusty fibreglass Abu match rod shuddered and creaked under the pressure and the 4lbs line howled in the warm summer breeze.

For a few seconds the tench became entangled in the

myriad of lily roots and weed that encircled my swim but then for some inexplicable reason turned tail and headed towards me.

Trying desperately to recover the slack line it occurred that this might be my best, and perhaps only chance, of landing this monster, so I quickly grabbed my landing net – small as it was – and tried to position it in the water.

My tench had obviously seen such an implement before and didn't much fancy the prospect of becoming enmeshed in its netting. "Go on lad, you've nearly got him," encouraged Ernie Nagle on the next peg.

Sinking the triangular aluminium head into the water I attempted to steer my prize catch towards it – in hindsight before it was ready. The huge fish was clearly far bigger than the net frame and merely lay across the arms thrashing about. Hoping the fish would drop into the net beneath, I lifted the handle with a sudden jerk.

At that point there was a loud crack, like the gunshot I heard last time I visited the Manor, as the thread on the landing net parted company with the extended handle. My float and line shot past my right ear and up into the tree foliage, before the net, plus my treasured tench, disappeared from view with a parting wave of it's paddle-like tail.

As the swirl in the water subsided I was overcome by a sense of total numbness, but could feel the anger and frustration welling up inside me. Like an erupting volcano I exploded. "Jesus, fucking Christ! You fucking bastard," I bellowed at the top of my voice, before sinking to my knees. I continued my invective as tears welled up in my eyes.

"Unlucky son," consoled Ernie Nagle sympathetically. But for the fact I loved my Abu rod I might even have subjected it to what tennis umpires euphemistically call 'racket abuse'.

I didn't bother setting up again, my heart wasn't in it any more. I just sat there wallowing in self-pity and then eventually spent the remaining minutes of the match packing up. I weighed in 17lbs 4oz, which placed me sixth overall, with which on any other day I would have been delighted.

As I emptied the contents of my keep net onto the scales, one of the committee men asked in passing, "was that you 'effing and blinding before?"

"Yes," I admitted, "I'm sorry, but I lost a five pounder at the net."

Norman Lonsdale had indeed run away with the match amassing 62lbs on the main lake, 33lbs clear of second placed Charlie Proudlove. However, I noted that had I landed that tench it would have given me sufficient for fourth place.

Though Ian didn't fish, I was the best placed junior and even topped Peter Cooke's 13lbs at the top of the arm, so it wasn't all gloom.

When it arrived though, the letter was quite a shock. It said: "Your membership has been suspended pending an investigation into the use of foul and abusive language within earshot of his lordship at the Manor. You are invited to attend a disciplinary hearing on..."

I was stunned.

Anyone who has ever fished a match alongside 50 working men will have heard plenty of choice language and profanities shouted – many much worse that the ones I uttered in my fit of rage.

My father read the letter and shook his head. "Well, if you can't keep your temper under control..." A phrase involving words like kettle, pot and black sprang to mind.

Nevertheless, father did do one helpful thing. He rang up the estate office and asked them if Lord Leverhulme had actually been in residence the previous weekend. It seemed not. A keen angler himself, he was salmon fishing on the River Tay in Scotland.

The following week I was summonsed to a kangaroo court at the club headquarters within the Men's Club, where the committee chairman read out, word for word, what I had shouted and asked what had provoked such a petulant outburst.

I explained about the lost tench, apologised profusely, and was then asked to leave the smoke-filled room while the committee deliberated. Outside I sat with my head in my hands, petrified they would expel me from the club. Hypothetically, I would lose contact with all my friends.

After what seemed an eternity, the door opened and I was invited in to hear their adjudication. Embarrassingly, my sphincter muscle was working overtime leaving a pretty loathsome trail as I closed the door. One of the committee screwed up his nose, and eyed me with contempt.

Looking over the top of his glasses, the club chairman cleared his throat and addressed me. "Peter, we have heard your explanation but take a very dim view of bad language on the bank side, and are particularly concerned this outburst was perpetrated within his lordship's earshot. We are very privileged to get access to the Manor lake and must ensure we don't give anyone an excuse to terminate the arrangement.

"That said, we have made allowances for your age and inexperience. Therefore, we have decided not to terminate your membership."

I breathed a huge sigh of relief.

"Consider yourself on 'probation' for six months. Have you anything to say?"

"Yes," I replied, cheekily pushing my luck. "His lordship must have bloody big ears to have heard me swearing by the lake. He was up in Scotland salmon fishing that weekend!"

Chapter 5
Irish mist

Given my brush with the angling club committee I decided it would be prudent to adopt a low profile for the period of my probation, and therefore relinquished the opportunity to travel on several of the club outings. It mattered not though as by that time Ian and I virtually had our own 'match group' drawn from boys at our school, and even a couple from the local grammar school, who we knew from the angling club.

Every Saturday morning around a dozen of us would meet at the station in time to catch the 6.30am train to Chester. When we planned to fish a stretch of canal more than walking distance from the station we even took our bikes with us, leaving them, and our tackle, in the guards van.

Apart from Ian, Tommy, George and I, the regular entourage from school included Steve and Mike Gurnell, Paul Armstrong, Barry Gordon, Stephen Lamb, Dave Bellis, Howard Winrow, Frank Duckers and the three Phillys, Pritchard, Parish, and Dalton.

Attracted by the big slab bream that inhabited it, one of our favourite venues was the canal basin at Christleton, just outside Chester, which we reached either by bus to the Troopers Arms or by cycling down the towpath. Casting to the reed beds and mounting a groundbait assault using catapults, Ian and some of the others, coaxed a few 2lbs bream from the bay. As usual, my groundbait either broke up in mid-flight or my Zoomer float became entangled in the reeds as a result of over-casting. Apart from small roach, all I caught was a huge water rat in my landing net, which the others tried to shoot, at point blank range, using an air-pistol. Tough cookies rats; the pellets simply ricocheted off its head. In those days we had never heard of Weil's disease.

Returning muddied to the main station in the evening bearing smelly wet nets, we could clear a British Rail waiting room in minutes. This included a 'brief encounter' with iconic British film actress Julie Christie. She was en route to Ireland via the Holyhead Ferry to make a film, but was quickly hustled out of the waiting room by her minders. Nevertheless, her incredible natural beauty certainly left its mark on this 15-year-old.

What started as merely day trips by a group of school friends ended up in quite competitive matches, mostly won by either Ian or George, usually with no more than a couple of pounds of small roach and the occasional bream. It was hard going.

As the weather turned, we switched our attention to running water and the River Dee, fishing sections near the bandstand and up on the meadows, even on days when snow lay on the ground.

Such conditions were a far cry from the following August when, in glorious sunshine, we fished the mighty River Erne on my first holiday away from my parents, over in the Emerald Isle. Up to that point, holidays had always been spent up in Scotland with my parents. Though I had fished a few burns, as they call small streams up in Scotland, with my mother's elder brother Sidney, most of the time was spent visiting relatives and family friends. I couldn't wait to be free to do what I wanted to do on holiday.

I think it was Ian's father, himself a native of Dublin, who suggested Ireland for a fishing holiday, while club member Jimmy Peers, in one of his rare helpful moments, pinpointed Belturbet as a specific destination. He also knew of a lady in the town who catered for anglers with bed, breakfast and evening meals. She even provided packed lunches.

A little reluctantly, my parents agreed to, and funded, the two-week trip in which Philly Parish agreed to join Ian and I. For some reason, now confined to the (Irish?) mists of time, Ian and Philly took a tent and camped in a field adjacent to Mrs Donahoe's white painted farmhouse by the river, while I, being 'indulged' according to Ian, enjoyed the comfort of a warm bed inside.

Despite that arrangement, Ian and Philly still took their meals with me in our landlady's large kitchen with its traditional range. A farmer's wife in her late twenties, Bridie Donahoe proved very welcoming, even though she had two small children in tow and another on the way.

Belturbet is 77 miles north west of Dublin, huddled alongside the banks of the River Erne in County Cavan. With a population of no more than a few thousand, it is a long main street punctuated with bars and a few shops, leading to an imposing grey town hall and church on the crest of the hill. From there a labyrinth of narrow streets leads downhill to the river and the bridge.

Freed from the shackles of parental control, we took full advantage of the abundance of hostelries, which, considering none of us had reached the age of majority, made us surprisingly welcome.

No one, including the one and only local Guarda took any notice of us – or the licensing hours for that matter. At 11.00pm the bar 'closed' and everyone filed out, waited ten minutes, and then returned via the back door.

Dressed in our 'mod' gear, including Ben Sherman shirts and Como shoes, we undoubtedly looked older, and were certainly way ahead of the local lads in terms of fashion – which may explain our popularity with the local colleens at the weekly dance.

Having experienced a few discos at home, a dance hall featuring an Irish show band, complete with middle-aged poseur wearing wellies, was a novelty to behold. Never before had we encountered a dance where all the girls stood on one side and the lads on the other. When the band leader cried 'take your partners', it was a case of grabbing the girl you fancied, but even if she appeared to like you, she would still return to the 'cattle market', as Ian called it, after just three dances and then you had to retrieve her again!

In the Diamond Bar, we met Bill, a tackle dealer from Tamworth, who had been visiting Belturbet for years and was able to enlighten us regarding every worthwhile stretch on the river and advise on bait and tactics. Bill could best be described as an 'amiable rogue', and after one drunken binge on Guinness and Smithwicks' bitter, blew up a contraceptive, which he just happened to carry in his wallet in case of 'emergencies', and tied it to the flag pole adjacent to the church in place of an Irish tricolour.

Though we didn't witness it, Bill claimed the priest was out early the following morning with his air rifle. In one of his less mischievous acts, Bill pointed out two of the best stretches of the river, one called the 'creamery' and the other known as the 'barracks', and we therefore decided to concentrate our efforts at these two locations. The 'barracks' held bream to around 7lbs, though the biggest we ever caught, using legering and laying on tactics, was in the 4lb region.

Procuring bait was a problem, but the local kids were only too happy to sell you a tub of fat lobworms, and big bags of breadcrumb could be bought from McMahon's chandlers shop in Belturbet, which also sold the most basic of fishing tackle.

I particularly liked the look of the weir pool just below the town bridge and set out to fish it one morning after Bill told me it was home to some big roach and perch.

Using my Abu Rod and 505 reel, I trotted the swirling, frothy water, which looked for all the world like Guinness itself, using a bulbous balsa float with a big lobworm as bait. Having caught several pristine roach and perch averaging half a pound, I was fully expecting another when my float suddenly held up in the flow, bobbled twice, and then slowly disappeared from view completely.

Initially, it felt as though I had snagged the bottom. Trying to pull the hook free I was amazed when the line suddenly scooted across the weir pool tearing line from my reel and it dawned I was connected to a very large fish.

Taking the strain to my left, I was extremely conscious of the limitations of my match rod. Whatever it was, a 4lbs line and a size 16 hook would not get it in. But one of the benefits of fishing a weir pool is that fish really have only one way to go in such circumstances.

Though they certainly pull in the strong flow they aren't going to leap the weir – unless of course, it was a salmon. No, surely not on the Erne, I told myself.

Gradually, I gained line, taking my time as the fish ploughed around in ever decreasing circles, eventually tiring and revealing itself to be an enormous – in my eyes – pike of at least 10lbs.

By this time I had quite a crowd of locals watching behind me. "Do you not have a gaff laddie?" said a soft Irish voice from the bridge.

"No," I replied.

"Well, you wait there and 'aul get one for yer."

Where did he think I was going to go?

A few minutes later, my new best friend appeared at the waters edge alongside me holding a gruesome looking implement with a splayed hook on the end. As he waved it towards the pike's head, the fish opened its enormous jaws and the line suddenly went slack. With an angry swipe of its crimson tail, it recoiled and headed off into the swirling vortex of water in front of me. Expecting to find the line severed by the pike's teeth, both my audience and I were amazed to find a roach of about 8oz on the hook. Closer examination revealed the roach's dorsal fin to have been crushed and bloodied by the force of the pike's jaw. "Be Jezzus," said my new companion with a wry smile, "You almost had two fish for the price of one. Mind you, no bugger would take my dinner off me without a fight and I suspect a pike is no different."

In all the excitement of trying to land the pike I hadn't noticed that the black plastic handle on my reel had worked loose and dropped into the river as I put my rod down. After consulting the owner of the chandlers shop in Belturbet we decided the only thing to do was travel to Cavan, 11 miles away, where there was a large, fully stocked fishing shop, that also sold maggots.

With my empty bait tins inside a canvas shoulder bag, we caught the hourly bus service from outside the

Town Hall and arrived in Cavan late afternoon. Sure enough the shop was able to produce a solution to my problem and with the bait tins filled to the brim, we had a couple of quick pints in a pub before heading back to the bus station.

Not realising the time, we found ourselves stranded as the 'bus service' terminated at 5.30pm. "We'll hitch a lift, no problem," said Ian reassuringly and we set off walking towards Belturbet, waving our arms with clenched fist showing thumbs up.

The first sign we came upon said, Belturbet 9 miles. The second claimed it was 10 miles to Belturbet, and the third, less than a mile later, told us Belturbet was just 7 miles away. Whatever the mileage, it was one hell of a walk. Not a single car stopped to offer a lift but everyone gave us a friendly wave.

Footsore and exhausted, we told Mrs Donahoe of our route march from Cavan. She laughed, "If youz want a lift here you just step out and people will stop. No one understands this thumb business, they probably thought you were wavin' to them."

After a refreshing cup of tea, I went to put my bait tins in the tackle shed only to find them both empty with the covers off. Just a few maggots remained in the sawdust at the bottom of the shoulder bag. The rest had made their escape through the air vent holes as I was trudging down the Cavan to Belturbet road.

On the Thursday night proceeding our departure from Belturbet we decided to night fish a spot Bill had recommended, two miles downstream from the town centre, which was regarded as one of the best bream holding areas on the Erne. Bill even arranged for one of his contacts to take us there by boat, as it was a formidable hike with the gear and groundbait. Before it flows into Lough Erne, the river near Belturbet is fairly broad with twists and turns through lush green meadows where cows and sheep graze. The spot we were to fish was on the elbow of a double bend in the river.

While Philly and Ian brought their tent, I had to be content with sheltering under my umbrella. Thankfully, it was a warm, humid August night.

As we set our stall by the slack water, and mounted a ten minute bombardment of orange-sized balls of groundbait, laced with smelly old casters and corn, we could hear the chug, chug of a motorboat engine, getting ever closer as it came upstream towards us. As darkness fell, we settled down for the night hoping the huge shoals of bream that nomadically patrol the river would find, and settle upon, the huge bed of feed we had laid down.

Throughout a disturbed night's sleep the motor boat engine could be heard periodically, each time apparently getting closer and closer, but never emerging round the blind bend and into view.

It must have been about 5.30am when I was suddenly awoken by the sound of a motorboat engine close by. "It's that bloody boat at last," said Ian, as we all sprang to our feet. Out of the blanket of Irish mist a small boat appeared on our side of the river and seemed to deliberately steer a course through the slack water we had pre-baited, so that it was no more than a dozen yards from our bank side encampment.

I called to the boat. "Hey mate, we're fishing there…" I never finished the sentence, for it was at that point I realised the boat was completely empty, yet was moving upstream as if some invisible figure were controlling the rudder of the outboard motor.

As the phantom boat proceeded on its journey Ian,

Philly and I all looked at each other aghast. "Did you see what I just saw?" quizzed Ian. Philly and I nodded in agreement, reaffirming the boat was empty. "Shhh," snapped Ian. The three of us listened intently. The motorboat engine had stopped. I turned to the others, "This I have got to see."

We ran along our bank for about a quarter of a mile, but there was no sign of a boat, either in the river, or pulled up onto the bank, and I reasoned that without mechanical power it would surely have drifted back downstream past us. At the very least, we would have heard the sound of oars thrashing the water.

It was a complete mystery. I felt a cold chill brush down my spine. Though we fished the rest of the morning – and extracted a few handsome bream from the swim – it was hard to recover my concentration and focus. I was in a state of shock.

Though it has occurred to us since then that the eerie engine noises might have emanated from an illegal potcheen still, or that Bill, ever the reprobate, went to a nonsensical amount of effort to set up an elaborate hoax, the over-riding conclusion is that we had just had a close encounter of the ghostly variety.

In the tiny Erne Bar the following night we recounted our spooky story. An old man, maybe 75, reeking of stale cigarettes and whiskey, with a weather-beaten and unshaven face, leaned over and spoke softly. "I reckon dat was Jackie McGrath's boat."

"Oh really. And where can we find him?" enquired Philly earnestly.

The old man fixed us with his gaze, and took another sip of his Old Bushmills, "Try the cemetery if yer loike, he's bin dead forty year."

Chapter 6
Top marks

Having thrown off the shackles of parental control during holidays, I was in no mood to be reined in yet again, but within a few weeks of my return from Ireland my father made me an offer I simply couldn't refuse.

Invited by the Royal Society to lecture fellow nuclear scientists at Cambridge University, he decided to make a full week of it by arranging business visits to companies in Stratford-upon-Avon and Kings Lynn, and to see an old colleague in Bungay, Suffolk. Normally, such an excursion would have held no appeal for me, but the common denominator with all these destinations, was that they were on, or near to, a famous river.

With the prospect of fishing the Avon, Cam, Great Ouse Relief Channel and Waveney, it took me about ten seconds to swallow my pride and agree to a holiday of sorts with my folks once again.

Our first stop was at the beautiful town of Stratford-upon-Avon. While my mother went shopping, father ensured I had the necessary day permits, bait and advice on swims from the local 'Johnny Parkes' before he left me, in a car park not far from the famous Shakespeare theatre, for his appointment.

The leisurely paced Avon was as pretty as a picture, bordered by immaculately tended lawns with benches, as it meandered through town. Several weeping willow's tenderly lapped the water's edge as their bows heaved to the slightest breeze. Standing up in a swim where a small stream entered the river, I fished for the rest of the afternoon, catching several fat gudgeon on float fished maggot, before switching to the swingtip and a lump of blue vein cheese, commandeered from my sandwiches.

Within ten minutes the tip rose and fell slowly twice before slamming around. As my old Forshaws Avon rod bent into a curve reminiscent of hooking the seagull in Ian's garden, I tried not to panic applying just sufficient pressure and was soon ready to slip the net under my very first chub of a pound or so in weight. Just then, I was conscious of a foul smell, and looked down to see several turds at my feet, lodged between my wellies. It was then that I realised my small stream also doubled as an open sewer outlet!

Our second stop, the tree-lined River Cam, which wends its way past all the historic colleges in Cambridge, was somewhat narrower, and more pedestrian, than the River Avon. It also had a deal more river traffic. Twice during the day I had to contend with long-haired student types, "beatniks" my father called them, seemingly worse for the effects of drink, either falling or diving in, from their punts, right in front of me.

Perhaps it was just me laying the blame for my own shortcomings at the door of all those silly punts, but once again the only thing I could catch was gudgeon.

My father gave me the choice of another day on the Cam or two days on the Great Ouse Relief Channel near Kings Lynn. The decision to leave Cambridge to the academics and 'beatniks' was an easy one.

For those unaware, the Great Ouse Relief Channel was excavated in the 1950s to relieve flooding on the tidal section of the River Ouse and extends almost 12 miles from Kings Lynn to Denver Sluice. Almost 100 yards wide, it is fairly straight and devoid of features, but in 1967 was regarded as one of the country's premier match venues because of its vast shoals of bream – that, of course, before some bright spark introduced Zander.

After buying a day ticket, plus a pint each of gozzer and annato maggots from a shop in Kings Lynn, my father and I headed off to an area between St German's Bridge and Magdelan Bridge, not far from Stetchley. Given it was quite a hike from the road, I was glad I decided to squeeze my trolley into the car for the trip.

Eventually, we found an inviting looking area where anglers had flattened the rushes into the shallows. My father left me at this point, promising to return around 5.00pm.

Told in the tackle shop that the river was 12ft deep with a weedy bottom, I followed their advice and set up a large Arlesey bomb paternoster rig with two gozzer maggots as bait. However, the man in the shop said cast, and groundbait, two thirds across the river. Obviously, he didn't know me.

Without the accurate groundbaiting to concentrate the fish, my rather pathetic tally for the day was one skimmer and one eel. Undeterred, I resolved to adopt a different strategy the following day. Choosing a swim about 200 yards from Stow Bridge, I set up my swingtip with the intention of fishing only two-rod lengths out.

This I could groundbait with some degree of accuracy. With two decent bream in the net after an hour I was relatively confident I had got it right, but my attention was distracted by the voice of another angler on the next peg, and what I can only describe as the most deadly accurate groundbait bombardment I have ever witnessed.

From where I was seated, every orange-sized ball seemed to hit the angler's float halfway across the channel. I went to investigate. To my delight, I found myself watching Leicester matchman Ivan Marks. His mate, Dave Downs, was on the next peg. They were practising for a forthcoming big match. Recognising Ivan straight away, from pictures I had seen in *Angling Times*, I asked if he minded me sitting behind him.

"Not at all," he chirped, "just as long as you don't tell them buggers from Nottingham what we're up to."

Ivan was the consummate all-round match angler. Never before had I seen anyone groundbait the swim he was fishing six-rod lengths out – with such deadly accuracy. And with his 'wrong' hand. Then, when he cast, his large Zoomer float found the same spot every time, almost as if it were laser-guided. As the float settled, Ivan hit bites I couldn't even see, to bring a succession of hefty bronze bream to his net.

I must have asked a hundred questions, but if I was disturbing, or annoying him, he did not show it, and though he rarely turned to talk directly to me, he answered every question with honesty and good humour, and even showed me his set-up.

I was in awe of him at the time, and still am to this day. He was quite simply the finest angler, with a rod and reel, I have ever watched – and that includes modern day experts like Keith Arthur, Bob Nudd and Bob James. If only some of the grumpy, self important, 'big time Charlies' I occasionally come across fishing open or team event matches today had such an easy going and helpful manner.

Years later I met Ivan again on the NFA stand at Birmingham NEC, and though now he was in his late 60s, he hadn't changed, and talked my head off for fully

40 minutes! Sadly, he died in December 2004 at the age of 68.

Inspired by Ivan, I eventually returned to my peg and caught another three bream before my parents turned up. My father said I was so excited he thought I had just heard from ERNIE, the premium bond computer. I even rang Ian from a phone box to impart my news. "You'll never guess who I've just met…"

Any notion that my brush with angling genius would somehow transform both my ability, and fortune, was quickly dissipated though when we reached our final destination of the week.

According to the guide books, the sleepy little Suffolk town of Bungay, had been home to Chaucer, and offered some of East Anglia's best fishing on the ponderous and winding River Waveney, which reputedly held bream to 7lbs, tench to 6lbs, chub to 5lbs, and best of all, roach over 2lbs.

Told there was a free stretch of river nearby, I was directed to a length about 200 yards from the town centre where the river dissected a park with football pitches and a meadow. "You trot bread down the inside and you'll surely get the chub and roach, even in the afternoon," said a local I spoke to as I walked along the high grassy bank. Cut fairly deeply into the meadow, it was abundantly clear I would have to fish the Waveney from a more elevated position than I would have preferred. The alternative was to scramble down the muddy bank and stand in the water. Landing fish could be a problem though, I thought.

Despite my reservations, I found a pinch of bread on a size 14 hook brought me several modest roach when I held back my crow quill float in the gentle flow, but the chub were conspicuous by their absence.

Perched on my box virtually at the top of the bank I was rather enjoying myself in this picturesque location. Almost imperceptibly, I noticed tiny lumps of soil rolling down the bank and splashing into the water. Before I had time to react, the whole section of bank upon which I was seated, slid slowly, yet deliberately, down the 45 degree slope, like one of those stair-lifts the late Thora Hird used to advertise, and deposited me, plus my new Berwood box and rod, into the water up to my knees!

Though not in danger of drowning this time, it was nevertheless a scramble to get the box, rod, landing net and myself, back up the bank. Though nothing other than my bait boxes and a rod rest was lost, everything was soaked and covered in mud.

Totally dishevelled, I must have looked like a mud wrestler as I wearily trudged back to the car park in the town where I had arranged to meet my parents. I was so caked, my father directed me to a garage where he hosed me down with clean water. I was then sent into a putrid public toilet to change into clean clothes. It was a long and silent journey home. "I don't think you're cut out for fishing," observed my long suffering mother.

Nevertheless, inspired by meeting Ivan, I resumed fishing club matches and even managed to finish second at Buckley Flash with the princely haul of 12 ounces, and for a time, I wondered if I could really cut it in match fishing. What a silly notion!

In reality, I was way behind Ian, who had already won three senior club matches, the Cheshire Association of Boys' Club Final on the River Weaver, and the President's Cup match at the Manor. And he wasn't yet 17!

George Taylor meanwhile, had fished the Liverpool

and District AA Coronation Cup on the Dee in Chester and had finished a creditable 15th out of 380 anglers.

A few weeks after our East Anglian jaunt, my father's' profession took him on one of his periodic trips to Belgium, but instead of returning with the usual box of handmade chocolates, this time he proudly produced a... roach pole!

Apparently, father had watched some Belgian match anglers fishing a wide, navigable canal, with long poles. Apart from that which they were using, each angler had several other poles of varying lengths set up vertically behind them, like canes in a hop field, each secured by spikes into the ground. Fascinated, my father asked the anglers, in pidgin French, to show him how the arrangement worked. It seems the poles were made of hollow fibreglass, and were up to 30ft long. There was no reel, so the tiny float, line, shot and hook, which came on a little carrier, simply fixed onto an spring clip at the end of the flick tip. My father said the Belgians whipped out small fish at incredible speed.

Spellbound by his report, I unpacked the Lerc pole, which was 24ft in length, and then examined the plastic rig carriers with their tiny white tipped floats – exactly like today's dibbers – and minute, size 24, hooks. My father had also purchased several packets of ready-tied hooks to nylon in sizes 22, 24 and 26. At the time, the smallest hook you could buy in this country was size 20.

When fully set up, the telescopic pole was both heavy and unwieldy, particularly with the metal spike in the butt end, but I did my best to learn how to handle it on the canal over the following weeks. I got some very strange looks from other fishermen, but Ian and, in particular, that progressive thinker Peter Cooke, were immediately struck by its potential. So much so, he bought one himself the following year.

Essentially, the pole was what we would call today, a whip, with a tip designed to absorb the shock of lifting fish out to hand. As far as I could see, it might be dodgy though if you hooked a decent bream or tench.

Despite acerbic comments from other anglers like, "can't you afford a reel mate?" or "is that your mam's washing line prop?", I still felt confident enough to use it when I entered the massive Crewe and Nantwich Round Table match in mid October.

One of the largest events in the north west angling calendar, it was fished by 741 anglers in 1967, including the likes of Kevin and Benny Ashurst, over five miles of the Shropshire Union Canal at Barbridge, near Nantwich.

My father drove Ian and I to the match, while George, now the proud owner of his own car, took Steve Gurnell and Tommy. Having assembled at the NFU site for the draw, I paid my entrance fee and pools, and even had a bet with a bookmaker who generously gave me odds of 250–1. I didn't reckon my chances were *that* good!

Drawn on a featureless section of canal at Wardle, I set up my Abu Mark 5 and the roach pole, fitting it with one of the tiny floats and a size 24 hook. On either side of me anglers stared in disbelief. "What the fuck is *that*? A tank aerial?" bellowed the man on the next peg, laughing out loud so everyone could hear.

Feeling more than a little intimidated, I was beginning to regret setting up the pole. I resolved to give it an hour and if I didn't catch anything I would switch back to the rod and running line. Fishing to the far bank with a single annato maggot on a 24 hook I caught maybe 20 of the smallest roach you could ever see, for about

12 ounces in weight. Not spectacular, but what pleased me was that it was 12 ounces more than 'big mouth' on the next peg. He wasn't laughing now.

With a hook length breaking strain of '0.55kg', whatever that was, I suspected the day could end in tears. Not being too well up on continental metric sizes, my eyes told me a bream of a pound would probably snap me up and sure enough one of maybe double that did so. Still, for once I didn't blank like big mouth on the next peg, and weighed in 13ozs – the second best weight on the section. Local man Derek Wainwright won the match with 10lb 10oz of bream.

After dropping Ian off, I was still regaling my father with the circumstances of my extraordinary thrashing of the man on the next peg when we pulled into the drive alongside our house. As my father opened the front door, I started to unload the gear, unclipping the rod holdall from the roof rack and placing it at the rear of the car. First, I carried my box and net bag down the side passage to the shed.

Returning for the rods, I could only watch in horror as my father, having returned to the car for some obscure reason, started the engine again, and with a sickening crunch reversed right over my holdall.

In thirty seconds I had managed to transform a day of triumph into another disaster!

Chapter 7
Just like Ronnie Biggs?

Had it been one of my father's scientific experiments the result could not have been more conclusive. Quite clearly, a canvas and leather rod holdall, plus contents cannot withstand the crushing load imposed by a 1966 Hillman Minx saloon! Yet, miraculously my new Lerc pole survived the catastrophe.

While my Abu Mark 5 match rod perished in an explosion of splintered fibreglass, and the umbrella disintegrated into a bundle of unconnected aluminium rods wrapped in green cotton, my latest fishing tool, which thankfully would not fit into the holdall and was lying loose in its own cotton sleeve, somehow pivoted on its axis – possibly due to air movement from the car exhaust – and spun around so it was parallel to the car wheels.

Thus it was lying, completely intact beneath the car, when my father and I surveyed the wreckage of another Bishop family angling calamity. In those days there was no protective plastic tubes for rods, merely a wooden backbone sewn into the canvas over the full height of the holdall.

While the Abu rod and umbrella were beyond restoration, my old Forshaws 11ft rod, needed only an application of Araldite – my father's panacea for every breakage – plus another of Johnny Parkes' excellent whippings, to get it back into service. My father was also able to straighten some of the bank sticks and the extending landing net pole using his vice in the shed.

The loss of the Abu rod was hardly felt though, because I simply inherited its twin from my father, who nevertheless decided to claim for the damage through his insurers. In due course, a cheque arrived, permitting the purchase of a new 36 inch rib umbrella and rod. Given I still had the use of an Abu 13ft match rod and 505 reel for canals, I decided to match the Mitchell 300 reel I had acquired in Ireland with an Allcocks' 'Benny Ashurst' 12ft Trent trotting rod for river work.

With that combination in mind, I decided to attend an end of season club match, in early March, on the Severn – a river I had never fished – at an unpronounceable, godforsaken location somewhere between Welshpool and Shrewsbury.

Those who constantly moan in the pages of *Angling Times* about having to pay £23 for an Environment Agency licence which permits them to fish anywhere in the country, would have been in a state of apoplexy during the late Sixties, when every regional River Authority issued their own licence. Thus, when I fished on the Avon and in East Anglia, it had been necessary to purchase three different weekly licences to cover my fishing. Most of my angling on the Dee and Shropshire Union Canal was covered by a single annual licence, which if I remember correctly, also covered a small part of the River Severn that passed through that River Authority's territory.

It was the day before when Ian reminded me that the stretch of the Severn on which our angling club was intending to stage the match fell under the auspices of the Welsh River Authority, and was not covered by the annual licence I already possessed.

I phoned the scholarly Johnny Parkes for advice. Even though there was only two weeks of the season remaining, apparently, I would still have to buy a full licence costing 15 shillings (75p).

"You've got to be joking," I exclaimed. That was extortionate given it would run out on March 15th. Anyhow, I reckoned the chances of getting your licence checked at such an out-of-the-way venue were probably about 1000–1. To hell with it, I thought!

As usual, the banter on the coach was cutting, and the smell quite obnoxious, as secretary Charlie Martin wandered up and down the aisle reminding us all it was a Welsh River Authority stretch, and outlining the match start and finish times. As he passed each angler, amid a haze of cigarette smoke, the Sunday newspaper lowered momentarily for an acknowledging grunt or nod.

The Severn near Welshpool was quite beautiful but nowhere near as wide as I had expected. Nevertheless, it had a strong flow and was up about 2ft following several days rain up in Snowdonia. I drew on a bend in the river where a sunken tree upstream of me had formed a slack away from the main flow. Feeding a handful of maggots every run down, I was soon catching dace, roach and gudgeon reasonably regularly, though I did suffer some of my customary tangles when the wind caught my line leaving me with a 'birds nest' around the bale arm. I also found it hard to avoid my line twisting every time I wound in.

It must have been halfway through the match that out of the corner of my eye I caught sight of a man flitting from peg to peg downstream of me but heading in my direction. As I didn't recognise him as a club member, it wasn't long before the phrase 'river bailiff' sprang to mind. "Oh shit," I thought, I really am snookered now. By the time he reached me, I had concocted what I thought was a plausible excuse. I would simply show him my English river board licence, and plead ignorance of the fact we were in Wales.

A ruddy faced man in his fifties, he slid down the bank to greet me with a laborious, and pronounced Welsh accent. "Goot mornink young man, I ham from the Welsh Rivher Authority. May I see your licence please?" I blustered and lied, but he wasn't having any of it. For a split second it occurred to give a false name and address, but in the end I considered that futile, as he would doubtless check my name with the secretary. Thankfully, he did not attempt to confiscate my tackle, something I heard bailiffs were entitled to do.

After giving me 'notice of impending prosecution', he moved on, leaving me to work out how I would explain this one to both my father, and the inevitable kangaroo court at the angling club. They would surely kick me out this time. With my stomach churning through anxiety, the rest of the match, and weigh in, passed in a blur. As I loaded my box onto the coach, I approached one of the more affable senior members, Tony Tate. "Do you think they will boot me out for not having the correct river licence?"

"I doubt it," replied Tony with a broad grin. "Two members of the committee got their collars felt as well."

On the faint premise the bailiff might have second thoughts, or by chance lose my name and address, I kept quiet at home and just prayed nothing would come of my indiscretion. However, when a large, recorded delivery envelope arrived, addressed to me, I knew exactly what was in it long before my father, somewhat inquisitive, opened it. As the red mist descended, I decided it was time to beat a hasty retreat.

"Jesus, bloody Christ! It's a summons to appear before magistrates in Oswestry." he exploded. I proffered the same well-rehearsed excuse I had tried on the bailiff, but it fell on deaf ears as he gripped me tightly by the collar and drew me towards his blazing eyes.

"In four bloody generations, no one in this family has ever had a criminal conviction, and now you blacken the family name with an act of gross stupidity," he roared.

"For God's sake Johnny, it's only for not having a fishing licence," protested my mother supportively, "The way you're prattling on, you would think he was one of the Great Train robbers."

"Well, the way he's going, he will end up like Ronnie Biggs!" shouted my father as he disappeared out to the shed. "Do you think he means I'll end up on a beach in Brazil with loads of money?" I retorted sarcastically, once he was out of earshot.

Examining all the paperwork it appeared I could either plead 'Not guilty' and the case would go to Crown Court where I would have to be represented by a barrister, or plead 'Guilty' in the Magistrates' Court, either personally or by letter, and get it over and done with. I opted for the latter, and was duly fined £5 by the court in my absence, though it occurred at the time that the associated paperwork must have cost double that.

To this day it remains my only brush with the law, but for some reason when I have declared it on job application forms, as one is required to do, it provokes comments at interviews like, "I trust that was trout of character!"

In the days before the advent of open all year round commercial fisheries, you either found a sympathetic farmer with a pond, or packed away your gear until the glorious 16th of June. Near Chester, in a village called Mollington, we found such a farmer, who had more regard for his bank balance than he did for the ethics of the coarse fishing closed season.

Now at an age, and physical size, when it was difficult to get away with a half-price ticket, a day's fishing at Mollington cost five shillings (25p) but it was well worth the walk from the bus stop of nearly two miles down a country lane. At a time when we were often content with half a dozen small roach and a bream to show for a day's fishing, Mollington offered prolific sport by comparison.

Indeed, I well remember one manic day in April 1968 when Paul Armstrong and I both caught 40 tench apiece on worms, after sitting through the worst thunder and lightning storm I have ever experienced. Prior to the sky darkening to a deep cobalt blue amid rumblings of distant thunder, the lake had not been at its best with only suicidal gudgeon prepared to sacrifice themselves. As the wind whipped up and the storm clouds gathered, large droplets of rain pummelled the lake surface making it look like one of those hot, bubbling springs they have in New Zealand.

With deafening claps of thunder directly overhead, and forked lightning slashing angrily through the gloomy skies, Paul and I both abandoned fishing in preference to securing our rather flimsy 36 inch rib umbrellas.

From under his, Paul called to me, "Do you think we should get under those trees, or leg it up to the farm house?"

"No, we'll get soaked," I shouted. "Best stay where we are. Don't you remember what happened to John White?" John White was a Spurs' footballer killed by lightning whilst sheltering under a tree on a golf course in 1964.

However, little did I realise when I said it, just how prophetic my warning against sheltering under trees during lightning would prove. Within five minutes there was a blinding flash, concurrent with a boom like a thunderbolt. All around the lake the ground shook, while plumes of white steam rose from the puddles that had formed on the uneven bank during the rainstorm. The hairs on the back of my neck and hands stood to attention. "What the fuckin' hell was that?" shrieked Paul, as a smell of burning wood and flesh permeated our nostrils.

With heart pounding, I jumped from under the umbrella and looked around me. Through the torrential rain I could see the smouldering remains of a large oak tree, split down the middle, in the field just behind us. Lying near it were three dead cows, their scorched and blackened carcasses still on fire.

"Bloody hell," said Paul, with a sigh of relief. "That was close, too close."

I was still in a state of shock when another angler, in his twenties, joined us looking over the hedge. Trying to take the tension out the situation, he quipped, "I know it's a bit early in the day for a barbecue, but does anyone fancy a roast beef sandwich?"

When the storm finally subsided, the farmer came down to the field to inspect the burning remains of his cows. Those that survived the 100,000 volt strike were huddled in the corner of the field, clearly petrified. He led them into another field.

As a shaft of sunlight finally pierced the rolling dark clouds, the wind suddenly subsided and a perfect stillness fell across the shimmering lake, triggering a feeding frenzy from the resident tench. They just could not get enough of worm presented over red groundbait two-rod lengths out. In the next three hours Paul and I caught a succession of 'tincas' up to a pound and a half, plus a couple of handsome crucian carp to record our best ever catch at the venue.

As the glorious 16th approached that year I had more than fishing on my mind. It was exam time, and I was pencilled in to take several GCE O levels and CSEs, as they were then called, and consequently hardly fished for weeks on end, as my father ensured I revised at every opportunity.

When the exams were finally over the sense of relief was immense, and of course we didn't have to turn in to school any more.

Ostensibly in town with money to buy some new trousers and a Ben Sherman shirt, I looked in at Hitchell's fishing shop – a rival to John Parkes – before heading off to the boutiques further down town. There, standing at the counter buying bait, was Philly Pritchard, one of our fishing gang from school. He too had been taking exams, but unlike me had been moonlighting during the evenings, working in a food-packing factory to earn extra money.

After chatting outside for five minutes, Philly suggested a quick pint in the nearby Happy Valley, a pub renowned for its flexible opening hours and relaxed attitude to under-age drinkers. With money in our pockets, time to kill, and an urge to celebrate the end of our exams, we both knew there was no way this would be just a 'quick pint'.

Taking his newly filled bait tin with him, Philly and I found a quiet corner of the snug and ordered a couple of brown over bitters. As the afternoon progressed one round followed another, as we quaffed pints like there was no tomorrow. By the time of the 'official' afternoon closing time we were both, to use a modernism, utterly wasted. It was at that juncture Philly had one of his mischievous ideas. Feeling under the table he eased the top off his bait tin whilst appearing to re-tie his shoelace.

Within minutes the 'troops' were on the march in every direction, as we sidled into the lounge in a fit of schoolboy – which technically we still were – giggles. At that moment a barmaid brushing up the wooden floor spotted the hoards of interlopers and let out several blood-curdling screams. That was our cue to run for it!

They knocked down that pub a few years later – probably because the Health Department condemned it due to infestation! Though not quite an abstinent my father did not patronise pubs, so was not best pleased by the state of me when I finally found my way home, particularly as I had not a penny left of the money I went out with and had nothing, other than a hangover, to show for it.

There is however, a sad postscript to that story. About five years later Philly was working in London when he was knocked down, and tragically killed, by a Hackney cab. A top guy, with a brilliant sense of humour, he is missed to this day. Our fishing 'gang' was never the same afterwards.

Chapter 8
Feeling cosy in Belturbet!

They say there's many a slip between cup and lip and
that was certainly the case as plans were laid for five of
us to sample the delights of Belturbet and Mrs Donahoe's
lodgings for a second summer in succession.

With Philly Parish dropping out early on when Mrs
Donahoe changed the dates after discovering she had
double booked us, the Irish invasion force was to con-
sist of Ian, Paul Armstrong, George Taylor, Tommy
Bywater, and myself. But then George and Tommy
dipped out the week before the ferry fares were due
for payment, leaving us with two places to fill at short
notice or cancel altogether.

One of the youngsters who had joined our regular
fishing 'gang', Barry Gordon, enthusiastically grabbed
one of the places with cash up front, while Ian somehow
managed to persuade his then girlfriend, Christine,
(and her father) to accompany him and thereby fill the
other place.

Not particularly interested in fishing, like most girls,
Christine much preferred the idea of hooking a bloke
and was prepared to go along with a trip to the back-
waters of Ireland if it furthered that cause.

Like any self-respecting 17-year-old male, Ian had
other plans in mind, mainly centred around the sleeping arrangements for the fortnight; and Barry was told
that if Ian's cunning plan came to fruition he would get
a room of his own to sleep in!

But Mrs Donahoe, who now had three children and another on the way, was nothing if not a good Catholic lady of high moral standards, and was equally determined there would be no 'shenanigans' under her roof! Thus she ensured she was always in a position to interrupt every time Ian and Christine got cosy together, and even took to night-time patrols of the bedrooms using the excuse of "just checking to see you are all comfortable".

While Christine dutifully tagged along as we fished by day, she was much more at ease dressed up during the evening, when we prowled the local hostelries and of course, the weekly dance. Almost certainly, sharing digs with four teenage anglers who permanently smelled of bream slime, wasn't her idea of a romantic holiday.

Conversely, Paul, Barry and I were not exactly enamoured with having her on our tails all day, whingeing about how long we intended to continue fishing.

Consequently, the amount of time spent actually fishing was inversely proportional to Christine's patience threshold, and the opening hours of our favourite hostelry.

While Ian, Paul and I considered ourselves fairly capable drinkers, the same could not be said for poor Barry, a year younger than the rest of us, who was clearly inexperienced on that front. On our first night Barry perpetrated what Ian described as a 'projectile vomit' all over the room they were sharing. In the morning, Mrs Donahoe appeared with a scrubbing brush and a pail of soapy water and told an extremely embarrassed Barry he wasn't leaving the house until he cleared up the mess!

Meanwhile, the ebullient Paul Armstrong certainly

made his mark on Belturbet. Indeed, it wouldn't surprise me if some still recall his Mick Jagger impersonation on stage at the weekly knees up, but one particular incident is almost certainly now enshrined in local folklore.

After a fruitless morning session on the 'creamery' section of the Erne had been curtailed by a prolonged storm, there was a collective decision to abandon proceedings and adjourn, under cover of our umbrellas, to the Cosy Bar, until the lashing rain subsided.

Situated two thirds of the way up the steep street that connected the Town Hall square with the Kilconny Bridge, the Cosy Bar – which boasted of offering the 'Cosiest welcome in Belturbet' – had a distinct advantage over other bars in that it had a juke box with all the latest sounds. It also had an amiable and extremely voluptuous barmaid, named Mary, who was known locally as 'Cosy Mary'.

An attractive bleached blond of around thirty with an enormous bosom that seemed to defy gravity, Mary also had a propensity to wear skirts somewhat shorter than might be considered decent in a small Irish town.

Just as the sign said, Mary always made us extremely welcome even though it was abundantly clear we were all under 18. In Ireland, no one seemed to give a damn.

When the rain finally stopped drumming on the frosted glass windows, we left and wandered up to the shops near the square in a mildly intoxicated mood. There, we met one of the Cosy Bar regulars, a rather simple, but harmless, local in his mid-twenties, called Brendan. He was, I suppose, Belturbet's answer to 'Forrest Gump'. As always, Brendan was riding his specially adapted, disabled tricycle.

Following five minutes idle banter about fishing, the price of Guinness and whether Mary's breasts were the genuine article, Paul asked Brendan if he could 'road test' his special bike.

Seemingly happy to oblige, Brendan nodded his consent, and within seconds Paul was pedalling furiously around the square, virtually on two wheels. But then without warning he suddenly veered off and headed down Bridge Street towards the river.

Appearing to lose control as he gathered speed, Paul could be heard yelling to anyone in his path as he hurtled towards the Erne Bridge. Along with Brendan, we could only watch in amazement as he somehow swerved to avoid two parked cars before disappearing from view. According to one of the regulars at the Erne Bar, who was forced to jump out of the way, Paul narrowly missed the stone wall buttress of the bridge, and careered down the grass bank, before the front wheel hit a large stone and catapulted him head first into the river.

By the time we had run down the street, Paul was sitting on the bank, absolutely soaked through, but grinning all over his face and holding a half-pound roach in his hands. "Look what I caught," he said, as the man from the Erne Bar muttered, "Jeez, is dat eejit with you? He should be in a fecken' circus."

Fortunately, there was no lasting damage to Brendan's tricycle, merely a wheel that needed straightening, though Paul did advocate some improvements to the brakes. Even Mrs Donahoe had heard about Paul's escapade by the time we got back to the lodgings. "Are youz crazy? You could have been killed," she chided.

While most of our fishing the previous year had been below the Kilconny bridge and weir, we resolved to spread our wings further afield this time around and take in some of the upper reaches and surrounding lakes. Considerably wider, but quite low after a prolonged dry summer, we were delighted to discover a virgin stretch where the roach and bream had probably never seen a baited hook.

While Ian, as usual, battered the rest of us in terms of quantity – much to the delight of his doting admirer Christine – I was fortunate enough to catch the biggest bream of the trip; though, as you would expect, it was not caught in anywhere near conventional fashion!

Having laid a trap with my customary random scattering of groundbait, I was pleasantly surprised when a shoal of bream averaging 3–4lbs settled in the vicinity and set about gobbling up my worm and caster hook bait on size 12 and 14 hooks.

When my 'lame finger' swingtip pulled around slowly before suddenly dropping back, I was sure it would be another 'snotty' of similar size to the others. But this fish felt distinctly heavier, and more ponderous.

While there is no doubt their English counterparts come in like wet sacks, Irish bream certainly make a fight of it. After several minutes of delicate coaxing and steady pressure, a large bronze bin lid appeared on the surface and rolled around a couple of times before I was able to slide the net under it.

To my surprise, the fish was not hooked at all, more lassoed by the line, which had wrapped itself like a ribbon around the dorsal and pelvic fins. The hook was even neatly threaded through the brass eye of my bomb ledger!

"That doesn't count," snapped Ian, as the fish tipped the scales at 5lbs 2oz. "You're supposed to be using a baited hook, not trying to strangle them."

Having just about had our fill of roach and bream, discussion during Mrs Donahoe's generous three-course dinner centred on catching tench – a subject, judging by her pained expression, Christine found less than enthralling. Questioned on the location of the nearest lake inhabited by the species, Mrs Donahoe passed the mantle to her farmer husband, who drew an impromptu map on a paper napkin.

"I tink your best bet is Putighan, it's only two moyles away, but the banks might be difficult to fish from," he advised.

We set off to view the lake immediately after dinner. Armed with the napkin map, we left town taking the first right fork, signposted Butlers Bridge, and the second right down narrow lanes bordered by stone walls and overgrown hedgerows. Following the map as best we could we took a left and sauntered down a long meandering hill but still there was no sign of a lake.

"How much further? We must have walked three miles already," Christine whined predictably. At the bottom of the hill we came to a crossroads which thankfully had a signpost.

To the left, the sign said 'Belturbet 2 miles', to the right it also read 'Belturbet'! Clearly, we were lost. Across the road a silver-haired man of maybe 60 wearing a dark suit, vest, braces and wellington boots was leaning over the garden gate in front of a whitewashed crofter's cottage.

"Good day to ye' all, and where moyt you be off to?" he enquired.

"We're looking for Putighan lake", said Ian. "Can you help us please?"

Puffing deeply on his pipe, there was a pause for considered rumination.

"If I were you I wouldn't bother with Putighan, Dawson's lake is much better," he said, exhaling an aromatic plume of grey smoke into the still evening air. "Just keep straight on and go left!"

Confused by this Irish logic we never did find either lake, or those elusive tench, and headed back to Belturbet in time for a last pint or two.

Talking to some of the locals that night we learned there was to be a 'fishing competition' in the town on the Saturday and quickly decided to enter – that was until we read the rules on a flyer outside the Town Hall.

It seems there were cash prizes, and trophies, for the largest specimen of each species caught on the day, but to our horror contestants were expected to slaughter their catch and bring them to the Town Hall for an official weigh in at 5.00pm.

Despite the lure of big money there was no way any of us were prepared to participate in such a barbaric and unnecessary ritual. We decided to watch instead.

There were around 60 anglers dotted around the river, including some English matchmen, each fishing in their preferred style. Some fished the fly, others live-baited – a practice I abhor to this day – for pike and a few tried spinner for perch, but the majority adopted conventional coarse fishing techniques for the roach and bream.

At 5.00pm we wandered up to the Town Hall to witness the weigh in, and straight away it was evident the lure of cash prizes had brought out the worst in the local population.

There were decomposed bream with missing eyes, which had obviously been caught weeks earlier, pike that were so stiff rigor mortis had set in, and a trout that was still partially frozen! But the piéce de résistance was a perch which looked as if it might have made 2lbs which incredibly tipped the scales at 3lb 4oz.

Raising his eyebrows, the match official suspended the dead fish by its tail and shook it several times. Like a fruit machine paying out a jackpot, small lumps of lead cascaded into a neat pile in the brass bowl sitting on the scales. "Nice troy, Declan, but I wasn't born yisterday." We couldn't contain our laughter.

Though we weren't really bothered who won the silver pots, there was some hostile mutterings when it was announced three of the English 'mercenaries' had walked off with big cash prizes.

While we never experienced any outright antagonism – Ian was always quick to point out his Irish parentage – we did detect a slight change in attitude towards the English, as news filtered through of troubles between Protestants and Catholics in the North – or the Six Counties as the Irish prefer to call Northern Ireland.

While there were undoubtedly plenty of Republican sympathisers in and around Belturbet, the majority of the population maintained a humorous, if not downright quirky, perspective on the thorny issue of reunification. In the Cosy Bar one evening, we found ourselves in the middle of a heated argument between two men regarding the 'struggle for Irish freedom'.

Things might well have turned quite nasty had it not been for the timely intervention of Mary who read the riot act to the two protagonists reminding them discussion about politics and religion was banned in the bar. "How dare you involve these boys, they're moy guests." As the men calmed down, one said to Mary, "You're right bonny lass. From a business point of view, the troubles could be quite profitable for me. I've got hundreds of camouflage jackets and balaclavas in my warehouse and I should be able to shift them now."

Though I had tried my hand – unsuccessfully – with a pretty young colleen called Theresa McCann, whom Mrs Donahoe employed part-time to wait on and make our beds, to my amazement, the Cosy Bar was the unlikely scene of my first sexual experience with a 'proper' woman as opposed to fumbles with girls of my own age.

On the final night of our holiday, the famous five spent a few hours sampling Mary's Guinness and Old Bushmills and feeding the jukebox, before moving onto the Seven Horseshoes Hotel. Lagging behind the others, I still had a full pint to finish as the others left. I promised to join them shortly.

As they departed, Mary gave each of the lads a peck on the cheek and wished them 'bon voyage'. With only one other, elderly, customer in the bar, she asked if I would help her shift a barrel before I left. Of course, I was only too happy to oblige.

Like a lamb to slaughter I was shepherded into a dimly lit backroom and heard the door slam behind me before turning to meet head-on Mary's pouting red lips.

As her arms enveloped me in a lingering clinch and French kiss (which I was only too happy to respond to) she pushed my free hand down between our bodies, and onto her magnificent, shapely breasts.

For a few minutes, I thought I had died and gone to heaven and eagerly explored her curvaceous super-structure. Eventually coming up for air, Mary whispered in my ear, "Well, you've been gawpin' at my boobs all week and daft Brendan tells me you were wonderin' if they were all moine. Now you know!"

With my resolve to return to Belturbet next year well and truly stiffened, it took me a good few minutes outside to compose myself before I entered the Seven Horseshoes. So *that's* why they call her 'Cosy Mary' I thought.

For reasons now confined to the mists of time, it was 35 years before Ian and I made a sentimental return to Belturbet. The Cosy bar was still there – and virtually unchanged inside – but Mary had long since vanished. However, the town still has a special place in my heart, for it was there that I discovered there was more to life than just fishing. In short, the boy became a man in that small Irish town.

If only I had put what I learned to better use. In subsequent years I wasn't much more successful at pulling girls than I was catching fish.

Chapter 9
Fishing for an alibi

They say if you can remember the Swinging Sixties, you probably weren't there! That's as maybe, but I wouldn't want to be a teenager again.

Even if you could cope with facial spots and rampant hormones, it was all too easy to become distracted by a burgeoning youth culture of either 'flower power' or 'Mods and Rockers' – both centred on music, drugs, fashion and sexual liberation – which offered an alternative way of life.

Though I never indulged in drugs (I tried a 'joint' once and never bothered after that) it was almost inevitable my fishing would suffer. Now, this was not a conscious decision, it just happened. It's hard getting up at 5.30am on a Sunday morning to go fishing when you didn't get to bed – and if you were lucky, not even in your own bed – until after 3.30am!

Apart from studying and working part-time to earn extra cash, my growing interest in football and girls all combined to make huge inroads into my available 'fishing' time. Indeed, after spending all of my senior schooldays at a single sex boys' school, to be suddenly thrust into a mixed college environment brimming with gorgeous girls was like finding yourself in a sweet shop with ten bob in your pocket. Wherever you looked there was something extremely tasty in view!

So when Philly Dalton turned up at my house one afternoon with a Vespa scooter adorned with chromium plated lamps, guards and wing mirrors, I just knew I had to have one. For a 'Mod', as I considered myself, a scooter with all the chromium-plated appendages was the ultimate desirable accessory, and of course, girl magnet – certainly better than an old jalopy car. Thus I hatched another cunning plan involving missed buses, and tutorials, to persuade my father of the validity of having my own transport to reach college, seven miles away.

While he had his reservations regarding the safety of scooters, my argument was sufficiently powerful to overcome the doubts. Within a week I had spent some of my small inheritance from my late grandma's estate on a secondhand Lambretta TV 200, complete with wing mirrors and spotlights, from Barry Turner's motorcycle shop. In the days before wearing head protection was mandatory, most 'Mods' wore a beret but my father was adamant that I should buck the trend and wear a crash helmet. It would turn out to be wise council.

Owning my own set of wheels opened all sorts of avenues, from giving lifts to fellow student and first love, Jane, to 'posing' on New Brighton promenade along with Philly and a dozen or so other scooter owning mates. It also enabled me to go fishing under my own steam at last.

Around this time, the angling club was in a state of disarray, due to the desire of some of the more match-orientated members to enter a team in the new divisional 'Nationals'. The issue divided the committee and split the membership and consequently there were few working parties to ensure the waters were kept up to scratch. Thus, on the occasions I rode out to the roadside ponds, they were either blanketed in weed or choked by lilies and were, to all intends and purposes, unfishable.

With no particular interest in fishing matches or 'Nationals', I was all for retaining the status quo, but Ian, Paul and George decided to leave the club and form Willaston match fishing group along with around 25 others, including Peter and Eric Cooke.

From Ian's perspective it was undoubtedly the right thing to do, and he went on to represent Liverpool and District AA in Nationals, and fished for teams like Wayahead Tubertini, winning many matches throughout the north west, and on the Irish circuit.

His CV also includes an Embassy Pairs Final in Spain and an *Angling Times* Final.

But losing Ian as a mentor and fishing companion was a body blow to me. Every time I suggested an excursion to the canal or the River Dee, he already had a match, or practice session, pencilled in his diary. Nevertheless, we still went out together socially, often with Tommy Bywater, who was one of those lucky guys with the looks – or bare faced cheek – to pull any girl he chose.

I remember once going to Liverpool by train and Tommy made a bet with the two of us he could get the phone number of a gorgeous girl, sitting opposite in the carriage, inside two stops. He got his money! Another time he saw a beautiful girl reversing her car into a side road, and deliberately walked behind the car so she would knock him down. He got a date with her too. Tommy eventually went to sea on the QE2 and it was his proud boast that he had cleaned up with the laundry girls, cut it with the hairdressers, and was doing the rounds with the casino croupiers! How jealous I was.

With Ian, Paul and George now fishing matches almost exclusively, it was left to myself and fellow scooter owners, Philly Dalton and Steve Gurnell, to carry the flag for the old gang. With the canal in Chester and the clubs ponds largely a waste of time, we took to fishing the Lower Park lake – home to some good tench and carp – mostly mid-week when we had free periods at college.

We found it was best to fish the lake early mornings, as soon as the gates were open, rather than the afternoon and evening when all the drunks, weirdos and gangs surfaced. Though it never happened to us, we heard of other young anglers being attacked and having their tackle stolen, so it is a myth such incidents are a modern-day phenomenon consequent to the dissolution of parks police.

On the first occasion I fished a Sunday afternoon until tea-time, disaster struck, on the way home. With my box strapped to the parcel carrier, and holdall balanced diagonally across my shoulders, I was approaching a junction outside a girls' Convent School (what a pity it was Sunday) when a large saloon suddenly pulled out of a side road in front of me.

While it wasn't clear whether the driver saw me and thought he could pull out before I arrived, or simply never looked in my direction, I had no chance, and never even had time to brake. Though I tried to swerve to avoid a collision, I only succeeded in hitting the car broadside at around 35mph. Philly and Steve, who were following, were able to stop in time.

The impact was such I was propelled upwards over the car and landed in a heap, still with the rod holdall on my back, right on top of a dwarf ornamental fence that surrounded a small triangular plot of grass adjacent to the junction. Ouch! I still recall looking down to see one of the steel fence spikes protruding from my groin area and blood dripped from my jeans.

As I looked up, I heard Philly's voice repeating, "he just flew through the air, just flew through the air," and then someone started singing the Bonzo Dog Doo-dah Band classic, 'I'm the Urban Spaceman baby, I like to fly.'

The next thing I remember was waking up in a ward at the General Hospital with my concerned parents leaning over me.

Luckily, the fence spike just missed my testicles, but pierced my thigh requiring some stitches. Apart from that, I had two fractured ribs, a broken right wrist and left ankle, plus severe bruising to my stomach and groin area, but thanks to the much-maligned crash helmet, no head injuries other than a sore neck.

In all, I was sidelined for over three months and missed the mock A level exams at college. In an era before it became fashionable, I never received a penny in compensation, either for my injuries, my damaged fishing tackle, or the written-off scooter. If ever confirmation were needed of my perennial bad luck, it transpired the driver of the car had neither insurance, nor permission from the garage where he worked, to drive it at weekends. The police enjoyed a field day, but I didn't.

While recovering from my injuries, I decided to pack in college – against my parents wishes after being told I would have to re-take the first year – and look for a career in design or engineering with day release.

As the Swinging Sixties gave way to the Spangled Seventies, so my once cropped hair was allowed to festoon my shoulders and Ben Sherman shirts and 18 inch parallels gave way to beads, tie dyed T-shirts and purple corduroy flares.

After several interviews I was eventually offered a job as a trainee draughtsman with the local Electricity Board, which could lead to becoming a qualified engineer.

Based in a large open-plan city centre drawing office, with a good proportion of staff under 30, I quickly settled and was delighted to find there was at least one kindred spirit amongst my new colleagues. For reasons that will become apparent shortly, it is perhaps best I adopt a pseudonym for him; so for the purposes of this book, we will simply call him 'Billy'.

In his mid-thirties, Billy was a real angling aficionado, who enjoyed coarse, game and sea fishing in equal amounts, and over the forthcoming years we shared many sessions on a variety of venues. By this time I was also quite enthusiastic about football, both playing, and watching Tranmere Rovers and Everton whenever I could. Thus the majority of my fishing expeditions took place mid-week, Sundays, and, when my teams were playing away, over whole weekends.

Apart from a Mini which his wife drove, Billy also had a capacious Austin van which was ideal when we travelled to fish the likes of the Bridgewater Canal and River Ribble, and on one occasion, the embankment steps on the mighty River Trent behind Nottingham Forest's ground.

According to the diary, I caught a good net of roach whilst trotting caster down the edge, though I do recall losing loads of hook links on the snaggy bottom and dropping my watch – bought for my 18th birthday – in the water when the strap snapped. You could say time stood still after that!

Though I was never particularly successful on the Ribble, Billy and I had some success on the Preston Brook stretch of the Bridgewater Canal where I caught my first serious common carp, weighing 4lbs 4oz, though more by accident than design.

After hooking it on bread, virtually under my feet as

I was adjusting my float and shot, I recall running down the bank for 50 odd yards trying to halt its run, while Billy attempted to bring the boat traffic to a halt, like someone flagging down cars ahead of an accident.

Billy and I also had a weekend session fishing for the big bream that inhabited a massive Cheshire mere near Northwich but that was cut short in the most bizarre and comic circumstances.

On the side where we were fishing, a car park had been formed among the trees at the top of the bank mainly for use by anglers, but according to Billy, local courting couples also used it. Thus when we saw a saloon pull into the car park about 10.00pm and immediately switch its lights off, Billy, made a gesture inferring copulation, and we both laughed.

It must have been half-an-hour later when I was conscious of the sound of breaking twigs and branches which grew into a low rumble as if a log was gathering momentum as it rolled down an incline. Turning to my left I was astonished to see a Vauxhall Viva glide silently but inexorably past us, accompanied by screams from the occupants, and carve a path through the reeds, before sinking into the shallows up to the wheel arches.

Billy and I grabbed our torches and ran towards the car. It was hard not to laugh at the sight that greeted us. In the back of the car there was a naked couple, still basically in the missionary position. "Get us out of here before we drown," yelled the man while the girl screamed hysterically.

"Calm down, and don't panic," said Billy reassuringly. "The lake is only two foot deep around the edge. By the look of you two, the only thing you'll drown in, is love juice!"

It appears the bloke accidentally released the brake

lever with his foot whilst on his glory stroke. The two of them looked thoroughly embarrassed as we waded out into the water and hauled them, with some difficulty, through the open car windows, before wrapping them in our sleeping bags.

Certainly, the girl was no oil painting, and seemed to have more teeth than a tractor gearbox. Even more cruel, Billy reckoned her boyfriend had been pumping her up to use as a lifeboat! When we finally pulled them out, Billy drove off to find a telephone. The Fire Brigade weren't interested but contacted a garage to tow them out. Needless to say, we never caught any of those big bream and after a cold and uncomfortable night, without sleeping bags, went home.

As my fishing friends from schooldays all went their separate ways, I allowed my club membership to lapse, particularly as I rarely fished so close to home.

With more rods than Johnny Parkes had in stock, Billy had the right equipment for every angling eventuality. Consequently, over the next few years I tried my hand at both fly and sea fishing, mostly in north Wales, though we continued to frequent those Cheshire meres that were fishable on a day ticket.

One Sunday morning Billy turned up at my house and announced he couldn't go because of some domestic crisis at home, and asked if I would look after his fishing tackle. Though disappointed, of course, I was happy to help him out of his predicament, and he returned to collect the gear at about 7.00pm that evening.

When he came into our office the following Friday afternoon and again cried off the weekend's arrangements, I was livid, as I had already bought and prepared my bait for a trip to the Ribble. But what could I do?

Over the next couple of months, Billy pulled the same

stunt several times, often turning up at my house very apologetically, and asking if I would look after his gear, while the van went to a garage, or some such excuse. While my intuition told me something was awry, with a shrug of the shoulders, Billy dismissed the constant cancellations as an inevitable consequence of family life.

The real reason became apparent one Sunday lunch hour, when our front door bell rang. My mother answered it and returned with a quizzical look. "There's a woman at the front door with a small child, asking for you. What have you been up to?"

"Nothing," I protested indignantly and went to the door. A petite, dark-haired woman, about 35, announced herself as Billy's wife, and said she was surprised to see me, as she understood I was away for the weekend, fishing with Billy! Fortunately, she couldn't see Billy's fishing box and holdall in the hallway behind the door. "No, I couldn't go this weekend," I lied, "I had to drop out at the last moment, so he's gone with someone else."

Glancing at a notebook, she then cross-examined me about other dates during the previous few months.

When Billy returned for his gear that evening, I told him of his wife's visit and what I had said. Normally quite imperturbable, he seemed unsteady on his feet and had to take a seat in our front lounge. Ashen faced, Billy finally levelled with me. Just as I suspected, he had been having a secret affair with a married woman who used to work in the wages department of our office, and needed me to 'cover his tracks' at weekends. With the addition of a mattress, the back of the van apparently doubled as a mobile 'love nest' for the two them.

So finally, my fishing hit rock bottom. All I was good for now was to provide an alibi for a spot of extra-marital philandering!

Chapter 10
All at sea

For once, it was reassuring to know there was someone who had got himself in a worse tangle than me!

Though I cannot say with any certainty if Billy ended his extra-curricular activities, the fact is, he never again used me as an excuse for them, and even though I moved on in 1973, we continued to fish together for the next few years whenever the opportunity presented itself.

Being the only exponents of the noble art in an office of some 40 engineers and draughtsmen, Billy and I did attempt to re-ignite the flame of interest in some of our colleagues who last fished during childhood. One day, we took Scottie, Colin, and Neil with us to the Shropshire Union Canal near Beeston – a convenient location complete with a picture postcard canal-side pub for lunch.

By this time, I had my own car, a bottle-green Hillman Imp, which had cost me the princely sum of £325. Parking our cars in the pub car park, we set off along the towpath until we found a suitable spot where we could fish, and see our gear when we adjourned to the beer garden for lunch.

According to the diary, the fishing was infinitely forgettable, with just a few eels plus small roach and perch to show for our collective efforts, but at least Scottie, Colin and Neil seemed to enjoy the day out. Lunchtime was spent in the beer garden of the pub, but given I was driving, I restricted myself to just a couple of pints and resumed fishing ahead of the others.

Returning to the bank an hour or so after me, Scottie was, shall we say, in high spirits, and was teasing a horse in the field adjacent to the towpath by offering it a clump of grass, then withdrawing his hand at the last moment. Attempting to steer his waning attention back to the fishing, I took his arm and tried to lead him away, in the process turning my back on the horse.

Suddenly, I felt a searing pain in my back, just below the shoulder, which made me jump and shout out. It appeared the horse had reared up and bitten me, and when I took my jersey off the skin had been punctured, causing it to bleed.

The others were beside themselves, especially as I ended up having to have a tetanus injection in hospital when the wound, in the shape of a big set of teeth, was cleaned up. Mind you, as I would discover in about a week, it wasn't the only laugh they had at my expense.

Any angler will readily admit their car tends to smell a bit fishy after transporting wet nets, but mine seemed to be worse than usual that week. Despite driving around with the windows open, the odour got progressively stronger until it almost made me retch.

I decided to check the engine compartment and underside of the car. Tied to the exhaust manifold I found the well baked remains of a large bronze bream, which explained the smell of rotting fish which permeated my car when the heater was switched on to clear the windscreen. It seems Scottie and company cooked up this little wheeze having discovered a dead fish in the canal, adjacent to the beer garden, after I departed.

I never did totally clear the repulsive smell of rotted fish from my car, but for some reason stopped noticing it after another friend, Phil Harrison, was sick all over the dashboard on the way home one night. In the end, I sold it for something sportier and less pungent.

Phil was among several friends – going back to primary schooldays – with whom I spent a week's holiday in Anglesey during the summer of 1974 at a camp site near Trearddur Bay, that had a small spring fed trout lake alongside. While we went to the beach most days, when the others decided to play golf, I fished, and was able to provide an evening meal for everyone, with several brownies about 2lbs apiece taken on dry fly, and, whisper it quietly, worm.

While the fishing was everything the brochure claimed, the facilities on the campsite alongside left a lot to be desired, so guess who got the blame for booking it on the basis of its fishing potential?

Taken short on the lake around breakfast time one morning, I hastily retreated to the rather primitive wooden toilet, which stood in the corner of the field, in full view of the cluster of tents occupied by Phil, Geoff Hartley and the other lads, who were cooking breakfast. Leaning my rod against the rickety structure, and taking care to lock the door, I did what I had to do, and then pulled the chain of the cistern above.

Nothing happened, so I pulled again. Still it didn't flush, so I yanked the chain a third time, this time with considerable force.

With a metallic squeal of protest, the entire cistern full of water came crashing down around me, followed by the three wood panelled walls, the roof, and door, all of which fell outwards into the field, amid a cacophony of shattering ceramics, twisting pipe-work and splintering wood. Unfortunately, that included my fly rod. If it wasn't split cane beforehand it certainly was after!

As the dust settled, I was left sitting in the open on the toilet seat, holding the cistern chain in my hand, with trousers down by my ankles, in full view, not only of the lads, who were in fits of laughter, but other incredulous campers in the field!

If I have had a more embarrassing moment in my life I cannot think of it. Indeed, it is an incident I still get ribbed about by the lads 30 years on.

After completing my training, I travelled Europe extensively and briefly lived in London before returning to the north west, initially with Liverpool City Engineers, and then with the embryonic Metropolitan County Council, where I secured a post as a technician-engineer. It was there that I would meet my future wife, Maria, who was secretary to my ultimate boss.

Around that time, Phil, Geoff and another old mate, Ken Gouldson (we all lived near each other) decided to form a Saturday football team, called Glasshouse, and coerced me into becoming first the secretary, and then both secretary and manager.

While many anglers pack in and sell their fishing tackle at some stage during their lifetime, at no time have I ever made such a conscious decision. It was simply a question of priorities, and at that stage in my life, my blossoming relationship with Maria, together with gaining professional qualifications and running the football team, took precedence. Every so often though I did fish the park lakes, canal and river, sometimes with Billy, but increasingly on my own.

But without the 'craic', as the Irish call it, resulting from comradeship with fellow anglers, my confidence began to evaporate and I endured more and more blank days. I desperately needed to recapture the sense of anticipation, excitement and camaraderie I enjoyed during my early days.

I needed a new challenge, so when some of my colleagues in the County Engineers suggested a sea fishing expedition off Conwy in north Wales, it was just what the doctor ordered to restore my flagging interest.

It is truly extraordinary how the combination of a day's boat fishing, plus the opportunity to consume copious amounts of alcohol and food attracted people who had never wet a line in their lives. The first time we went to Conwy, we filled a small coach, and two charter boats, with a total of 24 anglers, which represented a quarter of the men who worked in the department!

The coach trip to north Wales was just like the old days with the fishing club, with plenty of banter and laughter. Liberated from the restrictions imposed by driving, we took crates of beer and sandwiches aboard the boats, which brought a rebuke from the skipper, who pontificated about the consequences of mixing alcohol and rich food with a heavy swell at sea. "I 'ope you lads are sure of your sea legs?" he warned. "It can get prit-tay rough out there."

One of the benefits of hiring a charter boat, complete with knowledgeable local skipper, was that all the tackle and bait was supplied.

Though I had fished from a boat before with Billy, for the majority it was their first experience of any type of fishing, let alone sea fishing. Of course, given my track record and inability to swim, I readily accepted the skipper's offer of a life jacket!

With a box of artificial lures (feathers) on board, our skipper took us almost two miles out of Conwy to a spot where he knew we could mop up sufficient mackerel just under the surface to enable us to fish for the real prize, conger and tope.

In order to attract larger species, and release a strong

102

scent trail, it is almost obligatory to use a whole mackerel, mounted on a large hook, 'flapper style', which means removing the fish's backbone, so it waves around enticingly in the tide.

Whether it was the bacon sandwiches washed down with lager, or the sight, and stench, of our skipper boning and halving mackerel, George McLoughlin was the first to go quite pale and throw up over the stern of the Bryn Allun. Alan Bridge followed him. And we hadn't even set out for the tope and conger 'grounds' yet.

With plenty of bait aboard, we sailed into a moderate swell and drifted over a wreck which our skipper assured us was home to some huge conger and tope.

On that first day they were nowhere to be found, however we did catch plenty of small dogfish, pollock, coalfish and even a few bass.

As the fish rolled in, and the beer continued to flow, one of our chief engineers, David Bush, a man who normally bristled with propriety, became steadily ever more ill, until he was eventually lying prostrate in the galley, emerging only to be sick at regular intervals.

His rod though remained tethered in a rod rest until someone pointed out that it was arched over and the multiplier reel was screaming for help.

Assisted by Allan Wright, David rose from the deck and found himself engaged in a ten-minute battle with a huge skate, of almost 40lbs, which proved by far and way the best fish caught by both boats. After the skipper had helped Allan and myself haul the huge fish aboard, David eyeballed his catch, and promptly threw up all over it! He then slumped to the deck in a heap and slept soundly until we docked that evening! For some strange reason no one fancied taking the skate home for the table.

Though several – including David Bush – never made the trip again, the rest of us resolved to make it a regular event and for the next six or seven years, around ten of us hired the 'Bryn Allun' up to half-a-dozen times every summer. Even though the weather was not always perfect, it was rare that we did not enjoy an excellent day's fishing and I eventually added sizeable conger and tope to the list of fish I had caught.

I also took to fishing from New Brighton promenade but the idea of eating anything that swam in the then polluted Mersey estuary was pretty repugnant!

My boat fishing expeditions were not confined to the trips we made to Conwy. A few years later, while on holiday in Cornwall, I decided I simply had to try my hand at shark fishing, and found myself in a boat with six Brummies, all friends in their sixties, a couple of Londoners covered in tattoos, and a chap about the same age as me from Belfast wearing a union jack bobble hat.

On a vessel specifically adapted for catching the blue shark that patrol the warmer waters of the south west, we set off from East Looe with high hopes – though the skipper neglected to tell us until we were on board that only two shark had been landed all summer. Needless to say, I brought my usual good fortune to bear and we never had a single run between us, but the trip was nevertheless memorable for other reasons.

One of the Brummies failed to find his sea-legs and was being violently sick over the side when misfortune struck. The top set of his false teeth fell out. While his mates couldn't stop laughing he spent the next five minutes lamenting his decision to come aboard this 'poxy boat' in the first place.

Unbeknown to him, one of his friends took out his

own top set of false teeth, and placed them in a nylon shrimping net. Swinging the net and handle across the stern of the boat he said, "'Ere yow are Cloive, yower in luck. Dem teef were bobbin' around on the surface. They hadn't sunk at all."

Toothless Clive grabbed the dangling net, unravelled the false teeth, and afforded them a cursory examination. "No, they're not moine," he said with a dismissive wave, and promptly threw them back towards his somewhat surprised pal whose late attempt at a catch couldn't prevent them skidding across the deck, through the drainage slots, and into the swirling depths! His pal's face was an absolute picture. The bloke from Belfast shook his head and turned to me, "And you English tell jokes about *us* being thick!"

During our courtship, I surreptitiously introduced Maria to angling by way of just happening to have a rod and reel with me when we stopped near a trout stream or harbour wall whilst touring the Lake District and Scotland. Though she shared in my pleasure at catching brown trout, she was less than enthusiastic about dabs and mackerel from Oban and Stonehaven harbours. By the time we married in 1977, she had declared fishing was of no interest to her and best left to me.

After somehow steering Glasshouse to a championship title in 1979, I bowed out of 'football management' as a new, parallel, career in football journalism and radio broadcasting, opened its doors to me. Invited by a Sunday league to become their press officer, instead of fishing, my Sabbaths were henceforth given over to watching, and reporting upon, the machinations of football teams at grass roots level. Initially just for the local paid-for titles, I ended up covering the Football League for national newspapers on a freelance basis. I was also recruited by both regional radio stations, including Radio Merseyside, where I worked alongside the current BBC sports presenter Ray Stubbs, producing and presenting a 35 minute tea-time Sunday soccer programme. Though excited by the opportunity, I recall telling Stubbsy that football seemed to be taking over my life and my family and fishing would surely suffer.

Despite the legendary clumsiness that has afflicted my angling and other aspects of my life, I always tried to be as professional on air as I could. But, on one occasion, I put my foot in it big time, earning an official rebuke from the then station manager, Ian Judson. After recording a rather hesitant match report that I wasn't particularly satisfied with, I grunted, "that's shite" at the end, which should have been deleted when I spliced in the top and tail at either end of the report. Of course, I made a mess of it, and when the report was broadcast that evening there was short pause before my voice ended the piece with "that's shite!" The boss's memo ended with the phrase "any more cock ups like that and you can always return to your fishing on a Sunday…".

Though we operated a tight running order, occasionally Stubbsy would note a few seconds remained and would engage me in puerile conversation to fill time.

One week he asked, "Peter, just how important is Sunday football these days?"

Without thinking I replied, "There is no doubt Ray, that Sunday is now the most important day to play Sunday football!"

The now famous presenter doubled up on air leaving me to bluster unprofessionally and wind up the show.

The next day there was another memo from 'Judders' in my mailbox. It simply said, "Go fishing – Tight lines!"

Chapter 11

Treating salmon
with reverence

As my secondary career as a football journalist blossomed so my scope, if not passion, to fish every week steadily diminished. The flame may have flickered for a few years but was never extinguished completely.

I have often said there were three Fs in my life, Family, Football and Fishing. However, for a period starting in 1980, when Kate was born, and then three years later when my son, Mark, arrived, family life took preference and consequently my fishing was confined to the regular boat trips off Conwy, mid-week visits to day-ticket still waters, and of course, annual holidays.

When we took our breaks in the UK, I rather selfishly tried to unearth a caravan park or cottage in close proximity to some good fishing. Thus, interspersed between trips to Spain, the USA and the Channel Islands, we enjoyed trips to country retreats and farms in Wales, Cornwall, Devon, Somerset and Scotland, where the sound of ducks and moorhens were never far away.

Though an angler rarely loses his skills (if he ever had any that is) there is no doubt that lack of practice leaves you somewhat rusty. Just as a golfer cannot expect to pick up his clubs and instantly recover his handicap after a lay-off, so I discovered, to my dismay, some basic skills had deserted me.

For instance, though I could still tie a four-turn blood

knot on a small, eyed hook, for the life of me I couldn't get a spade end whipping right, and it cost me some good fish.

While my casting was no different – it has always been atrocious – the lack of weekly practice brought about even more tangles than usual, and consequently increased the sense of frustration within myself. Indeed, I would be the first to admit I was not a good teacher to my son when he was old enough to learn, and that was purely down to a lack of confidence in my own ability. If you are wrestling with yourself, you cannot teach someone else with any degree of patience. Despite that, we did have some fun and games...

Staying in a cottage in Somerset, near Bath, which had its own small carp and trout lakes, exclusively for residents, I fished, and caught quite well, early morning and evening, so as to leave the day free for those family days out. But on one occasion I managed to persuade 'she who must be obeyed' that we could combine a spot of fishing for me, with a day out for the children to Longleat Safari Park, near Warminster.

Home to the Marquess of Bath, the Longleat Estate has three man-made lakes, which could be fished on a day ticket, for just £1. After doing our tour of the Safari Park in the car, we split up, and Maria took the children to the house, adventure playground, and aquarium, while I headed to the lakes, having been told tickets could be purchased on the bank.

Walking across well-manicured lawns, I plonked down my box and holdall beside an inviting spot on a large, reed-fringed lake, and started to assemble my rod, oblivious to all around me.

Thankfully, I have had few shocks in my life sufficient to engender momentary loss of bowel control, but what

I saw next very nearly brought such a reaction. Rising from a partially submerged position about 30 yards in front of me was the easily recognisable head of a huge hippopotamus, blowing water vertically through its nostrils to create a huge bow wave, which lapped the shore where I was standing. "Jeeesus!" I exclaimed with surprise, before the penny quickly dropped.

Just then a striped Land Rover pulled up nearby and a park warden got out. "Don't worry." he said sarcastically, "we wouldn't have let the hippo's eat you. There are also sea-lions in here and consequently no fish. We've been watching you from the lodge, trying to attract your attention. We wondered how long it would take before you realised you were on the wrong lake."

Pointing, he added, "the three fishing lakes are over there."

To say I felt stupid would be an understatement. I should have had much stronger line on my reel than 4lbs breaking strain if I wanted to land one of those hippos.

After moving to the smallest pool, directly in front of Longleat House, I caught a couple of decent bream and crucians on corn so my three-hour break for freedom wasn't entirely wasted, but I had some story to tell the kids when they returned…

You would think I would have learned my lesson, but a couple of years later in Cornwall, I was again taken to task for fishing the wrong lake at a fishery, though this time, thankfully, there were no hippo's about.

According to the 'bailiff' in the entrance hut, the first lake I would come to down the track was a 'mixed' coarse lake and the second, a specimen carp lake. Having paid my day ticket, Kate, Mark and I stopped alongside the first lake we came to – though it was considerably smaller in size than I had anticipated.

Setting up two rods, each with a simple float arrangement and size 18 hooks, baited with double white maggots, I threw a handful in before casting, and was surprised to see them eagerly snapped up by fish cruising just below the surface. I promptly re-adjusted my shotting arrangement, so the baited hooks would fall slowly through the top layer of water.

Casting into the lake, I let the float settle and then handed the rod to Kate. Within seconds the float disappeared and the line went taut. "Go on," I said. "Strike and wind him in." Though she held the rod at arm's length, as if it was likely to poison her, within a few turns of the handle a small rainbow trout was thrashing about on the bank. After unhooking, I encouraged her to hold it before I released it back into the water.

Next cast I handed the rod to Mark, who must only have been about four, and when the float went under held the rod as he wound the handle on the reel. Once again a small trout bounced around on the grass in front of us.

Either this lake is truly 'mixed' or we're on the wrong pool, I thought. In the next half-hour we must have caught around a dozen small brown and rainbow trout and the best two, each of about a pound and a half in weight, went into my bag!

The kids loved it, and both had their pictures taken holding their first ever catch. Of course, it wasn't long before we were rumbled. The bailiff turned up yelling, "What the hell do you think you're up to, that's the trout stock pond you're fishing."

I just acted daft – something I find comes quite easily at times – replying, "Well, *you* said the first lake I would come to is a mixed lake, and that the one I'm fishing. I've never been here before, so how am I supposed to know the difference between this lake, and the coarse lake, which you now say is further down the lane!" It was just like the old Monty Python 'I've come for an argument' sketch!

In the end we moved, but the much larger 'mixed' coarse lake was nowhere near as much fun! I returned later in the week, with a teenager named Garry Doolan, who was staying in the next caravan to us, and turned out to live not six miles from our home. I had a couple of small tench and a decent bream on corn, while Garry caught a carp of about three pounds on meat, and introduced me to some new baits and methods I hadn't encountered before.

In 1984 I was approached by Tranmere Rovers Football Club with a view to taking over as editor of their match programme, a position I went on to hold for 14 years. One of the people I recruited a few years later to cover reserve matches was young Garry, who pleaded for the chance to launch a career in football journalism, even though he was still at school.

With a little help and encouragement from me, plus no little natural talent of his own, Garry eventually graduated to the staff of the Daily Mail sports desk before packing it all in to become a policeman. To this day, despite the age gap, he remains a good mate and occasional fishing companion.

Having tried my hand – mostly unsuccessfully – at coarse, sea and trout angling over the years, one of the challenges that remained was to fish for salmon, something I had always regarded as elitist and financially prohibitive.

But that changed in bizarre circumstances one balmy August when we returned to my family's roots in the north east of Scotland to stay on Royal Deeside,

111

with a long term friend of my parents, Tom Proudlove. Tom and his wife ran a bed and breakfast near Aboyne, Aberdeenshire, in one of the most heavenly and tranquil locations you could imagine.

Over breakfast one morning, I was quizzing Tom about the best trout streams nearby when he suddenly said, "Och, do you nae fancy a spot of salmon fushin instead? I'll have a word wi' ma pal Wullie and see if he can fix it up."

Willie, it appeared, was a ghillie on the River Dee between Aboyne and Ballater, an incredibly exclusive section of river, close to the Balmoral Estate, which was world renowned for its salmon fishing. It was the sort of beat money alone could not buy an invitation to fish.

I listened as Tom spoke to Willie on the 'phone in the hall, but could only catch the odd word or phrase like 'Bishop', 'Birkenhead', 'holiday', and 'nae had a salmon before'.

Tom returned to the breakfast table. "Well, that's a' sorted oot for the evening rise. Do you have waders yoursel?" After telling Tom I only had an 8ft trout rod, reel, and net with me, he disappeared to the shed and returned with a set of chest waders, plus a 14ft long split cane salmon rod and reel, both made by Hardy.

"Yon rod is ideal," said Tom adding, "you'll need the extra length to cast at forty-five degrees, then mend your line and allow the fly to track over the salmon lies."

Almost as an afterthought he added, "Och, and one thing to remember the necht, whatever you do, nae bad language. Wullie is a very religious man and it would cause deep offence." I nodded.

It took us no more than ten minutes to reach the estate near Muir of Dinnet where the Dee snakes its way through forests and the snow-tipped Cairngorm Mountains.

The smell of resinous Scots pines and aromatic heather plus the sound of wood pigeons and running water all combined to create a unique ambience as we made our way through the trees to a wooden fishing hut alongside a large and languid pool. Overhead, a couple of kestrels circled before swooping upon their prey.

Like a character from a children's rhyme, Willie the Ghillie, who must have been in his sixties, was waiting for us with his faithful labrador, Sandy. Dressed in tweeds and deerstalker, he was the epitome of the traditional Scottish fishing guide.

I introduced myself as Peter, and shook hands, but somehow felt he viewed me with a degree of suspicion. Maybe he was like that with all Sassenachs I thought.

Tom meanwhile set up the rods, and from a box of brightly coloured flies, chose one called a 'blue charm' for me to start with. As we made our way across the shallows, I reminded Tom that I couldn't swim and wouldn't be comfortable wading up to my chest in the chilly and gin-clear water.

Wading out gingerly, so as to avoid the slippery boulders underfoot, I overheard Willie remark to Tom, "You say yon man is a Bishop, but I'm thinking he's a wee bit young to have risen to that high office." I didn't react, but when Tom caught up with me I asked what was going on.

With a twinkle in his eye he replied, "Och, he's wee bit hard of hearing, and when I asked him if you could fish, somehow he got the idea you were *the* Bishop of Birkenhead, not Peter Bishop from Birkenhead."

For the rest of the evening I did my best to maintain

an ecclesiastical demeanour as Tom treated me with utter reverence in an effort to keep up the pretence. Willie, I could tell, was not convinced, but as Tom observed later, he was such a snob, it suited him to be able to say he had acted as ghillie to the Bishop of Birkenhead.

Fly fishing with a 8ft rod on small burns is mightily different to casting a heavy line, double handed, with a 14ft rod, and after an hour or so standing up to my thighs in rushing water, my arms and shoulders were aching.

Despite Willie's advice, by 8.00pm neither Tom or I had seen sight nor sound of a salmon, which I gather is not unusual. Anyway, for once, catching seemed largely irrelevant.

Who could want for more than to be in such a beautiful spot as the sun went down behind the Cairngorms, casting a shimmering reflection on the river? The Scots call that time of evening 'the gloaming', and it is supposed to be the prime time to catch sea trout.

"Would 'your grace' care to try for a sea trout using a 'silver stoat's tail'?"

There was a trace of sarcasm in Willie's voice. I nodded graciously. Amazingly, with my first cast into the deep pool, I got a vicious take and the line screamed off my reel as the fish darted downstream. Excitedly, I shouted to Willie, "Do you think it's a salmon?"

Some ten yards away, he fixed me with a steely gaze. "Judging by it's fight Sir, I'd say that's nae more a salmon than you are the Bishop of Birkenhead!"

Apparently rumbled, I didn't react, but after teasing the fish upstream allowed Willie to slide his net under a fin perfect 4lbs sea trout, which glistened in the dusk. Reaching into his pocket, Willie asked patronisingly,

"Would the Bishop care to do the dirty deed, or

would it ease his conscience if the 'priest' administered the last rights?"

Unable to think of anything particularly pastoral to say in response, I procrastinated for a few minutes and then attempted an ill-advised humorous riposte. "Well, all we need now is another two fish and five loaves...!"

If only I had enjoyed the benefit of a public school or Oxbridge education I might have be able to say something more profound.

Willie glared at me. Tom rolled his eyes and looked to the heavens. "Oh, bollocks!", I muttered under my breath.

After tipping our ghillie generously for his services, Tom ushered me away and that night the *Bishop of Birkenhead* sought forgiveness in prayer as he and his fellow conspirator enjoyed grilled sea trout for their supper!

It just goes to show you don't actually need to catch a salmon to enjoy the fun of salmon fishing. Merely treat the sport with the requisite measure of reverence!

After enjoying myself up in Scotland I was even more determined to get Mark seriously interested in fishing. Conscious I would need to invest in some new gear, I decided to buy him a pole, on the basis it would be easier to learn with than rod and reel, and eventually settled on a 7 metre take apart type.

On Christmas morning 1990 Mark seemed well pleased with his present, but by afternoon it was completely useless, after he innocently pulled the fourth section through the fifth – thinking it was telescopic – to leave it totally wedged together.

Despite a lot of swearing and the scientific application of movement and heat, my father and I were unable to separate the sections. For once at Christmas we would have preferred to be 'poles apart' rather than 'up the pole'!

With the pole consigned to the dustbin, when Mark and I next went fishing it was back to the trusty rod and line as we targeted carp.

Chapter 12
The King and I...

If you were to set your sights on catching really big carp you probably wouldn't choose the north west of England as a location. Similarly, if you actually lived on the border of Cheshire and Merseyside, you wouldn't *choose* to specifically target that species unless you were one sandwich short of a full picnic.

And so it was that I would switch my attention to the pursuit of leviathans in one of the least productive areas in England. In the south east it would appear most 12-year-olds have had at least one 30lbs, and for those more experienced 'specialists' – that word again – with access to the best syndicate and day ticket waters, fish up to, and over, 40lbs are a realistic possibility.

But everything is relative. Surely, a 20 odd-pound fish – particularly if it isn't known – caught in our neck of the woods has greater intrinsic value than one of those commonplace mid-30s from an Essex lake, that labour under a name like 'Mary' or 'The Dustbin'. Therefore, given the scarcity of carp over 25lbs in the region, I am not ashamed to say that 14lbs 8oz is my biggest when *specifically* targeting the species. I have had a larger carp but that is another story...

Having attempted just about every other branch of the sport, I suppose it was inevitable that fishing for carp would eventually captivate me, even though I was almost 40 before the bug bit. Of course, it was young Garry, by then working full-time as a football journalist, who introduced me to the art of tea making, reading, sleeping and cooking which masquerade as fishing for big carp. We targeted several waters that were known to contain carp over 20lbs, including Burton Mere near Chester, Egerton Fruit Farm near Malpas, and Hickory Hollow in Whitchurch, Shropshire.

Today a syndicate water, Hickory consists of three lakes stocked with mainly big mirrors plus smaller commons and grass carp. Set, as its name would suggest, in a hollow on the edge of town, it was overlooked on one side by the back gardens of a row of terraced houses, so when the fishing was slow, you could always listen to the neighbours rowing during summer evenings! One night a couple were going at it hammer and tongs in the garden, and during a brief respite, the chap on the next peg bellowed at the top of his voice, "Listen love, I think its time for you to go to your sister Susan's house." Intrigued, I asked if he knew them. "No, never met them. But they had the same row last night and she said, 'I'm going to stay at Susan's,' and he replied, 'What do I care? Go on, piss off to your sister's.'"

On my first visit to Hickory with Garry I caught a mirror of 10lbs 12oz in a scum-covered corner, 18 inches deep only a few inches from the bank on a big chunk of luncheon meat over a bed of hemp. It was a minor miracle I got it in, as it became totally tangled in the other line I had out. So much for fishing two rods!

For a week it was the biggest freshwater fish I had ever caught. Then I netted another whacker, this time 12lbs 4oz – again from the margins – and that was me hooked both on the venue, and carp fishing, especially as Garry said the lake contained a few over the magic 20 mark.

On the strength of my early success, I went out and

bought a carp rod, baitrunner reel, optonic bite alarm, and a capacious net to land all those big fish. However, the 14lbs 8oz mirror I caught at Hickory one perfect summer evening, again down the edge, was the largest fish that ever graced that net.

Because the banks surrounding Hickory Hollow were relatively flat, though occasionally muddy, on a couple of occasions we saw disabled anglers fishing there, even though there was no specific provision for them. The visit of one such angler, maybe in his late twenties, who looked as if he might be a cerebral palsy sufferer, left an indelible memory on all those that were at the lake that day. Taken to his peg via wheelchair by what might have been an older brother, his carer set him up with a rod set in rests alongside him, though it seemed unlikely he could even strike or reel in without assistance.

A cheerful, but somewhat raucous character, he certainly made his presence known to everyone else on the lake. As each angler landed a fish, including his brother and his mate, he bawled "Jammy bastard" at the top of his voice, much to everyone's amusement. Then late in the afternoon we heard his brother shout, "Tommy, you've got one lad, look at your rod, it's almost off the rest."

Garry and I, fishing virtually opposite, looked up from our newspapers. His brother grabbed the rod and screwed down the screaming clutch to bring the running fish to a halt. Handing the rod to his brother so the butt was trapped between his arm and the side of the chair, he steadily cranked the reel until the fish – a carp of around 6lbs – was thrashing around in front of him. He then let Tommy hold the rod butt, as he slid the net under it.

There must have been 15 people scattered around the lake that day, and as the fish nestled in the landing net, spontaneous applause broke out, followed by several voices – including my own – shouting "Jammy bastard!" in almost perfect unison. Even Tommy himself, could be seen chuckling, and, for the rest of the day, he kept quiet when anyone else landed a fish.

With only one carp rod and optonic, my usual approach at Hickory was to use my Avon rod to drop a simple float rig with 8–10lbs line and a big bait down the edge, and cast the other rig as near to the island as I could manage, and utilise my one bite alarm. This, of course, is where my legendary casting skills caught up with me. Either I dropped ten yards short of the island, or overcast and became entangled in the overhanging bushes, and pulling for a break with 12lbs line is no joke.

Thus, I perfected a technique where I would set up my lead and rig but leave off the hook link and then cast several times until I achieved the optimum range. I then clipped up and added the hook link with a boillie, luncheon meat or double corn as bait. The important thing to remember was to take the line off the clip afterwards or you could be in serious trouble if the fish ran around the island!

This worked well, though the carp around the island were invariably smaller in size than those caught in the margins, but inevitably the day would come when I forgot to unclip the line after casting...

As soon as I struck I knew I was in trouble, but could do nothing about it. It will surely try to circumnavigate the island I thought, but no, this carp had something quite different, and unconventional, in its locker!

Like an amphibious craft, it went straight up the

sloping bank of the island and into the undergrowth, briefly revealing itself to be a long cigar-shaped grass carp of maybe 8 or 9lbs, before rolling back into the water with a huge splash and shedding the hook. Somehow, it even managed to leave me attached to a submerged tree stump on the edge of the island.

If that wasn't bad enough, later the same day a duck decided to grab a large cube of luncheon meat which I had placed in less than two foot of water in the margin to my left. Now, most anglers surface fishing have hooked a duck at some time, but on the bottom? I ask you! Obviously attracted by the bed of corn, trout pellets and hemp seed with which I had laid a trap for the cruising carp, Daffy Duck had been sticking its head under water and found the meat on the shelf. The particularly vocal commotion in the water to my left alerted me immediately to what had happened, as the tethered bird flapped around trying to take off.

At first I gave it line, amid contradictory advice from several well-meaning anglers close by, but then decided the kindest thing to do in the long run was wind in and extricate the poor bird from the hook. But every time I drew it close enough to net, it panicked and attempted to fly off again.

Much to my chagrin someone opposite decided to 'commentate' with a brilliant parody of Donald Duck, which set off everyone else laughing. Eventually, Garry scooped the duck into the net but not before it snapped the tip of my Avon Rod, thereby necessitating a six-inch truncation.

Within a minute we were able to release the bird unharmed and seemingly none the worse for its ordeal, though I did wonder what it might look like covered in orange sauce and surrounded by new potatoes and garden peas!

Another Bloody Tangle!

Having taken a week's holiday with the intention of visiting a new water every day, I stumbled upon a beautiful and incredibly tranquil day ticket venue called Harthill, near Broxton, in Cheshire. Comprising three near 200-year-old estate lakes, the top lake was reserved for fly fishing, though it was said there were wild carp and big tench in there, while the bottom two secluded pools, at the end of a ¾ mile long leafy lane, contained bream and common carp.

Hidden in a valley with a cliff on one side, and shrouded by tall pines, with only the sound of woodpeckers and cuckoos for company, the banana shaped rock pool was the perfect retreat from civilisation.

Having never fished Harthill before, I tried the usual baits such as meat, corn and dog biscuits, but was looking at another blank until the very helpful lady owner, Fiona, appeared. She told me some big carp – including the biggest fish in the pool – were basking up in the shallows at the top end and might be tempted with free-lined floating crust.

When I told her I only had biscuits, she hurried off, re-appearing ten minutes later with a half a crusty loaf. By that time I was creeping along behind some blackberry bushes, peering over the top at a shoal of large commons basking, almost motionless, in about 18 inches of water, enjoying the mid-day sunshine on their broad golden backs. Occasionally, they turned slowly and deliberately through 90 degrees, like submarines, their dorsal fins standing proud above the water line looking, for all the world, like periscopes.

Every so often a large mouth broke the surface film to hoover up a fly or some other floater off the surface, but generally they seemed quite lethargic, and probably disinterested in feeding.

At a guess, the biggest fish in the group, whom I decided had to be the king of the pool, must have been between 18–20lbs, while his entourage were all in the 8–12lbs range. Thankfully, they all seemed oblivious to my stilted presence.

Tearing a piece of crust from the loaf, I threw it up and over the bush and then rose from my crouching position to see if there had been any interest. The crust had landed not two feet from the King's nose, yet he showed no inclination to feed whatsoever. I threw several others pieces, and was eventually delighted to hear that telltale slurping noise. It was time to try with a baited hook so I returned to my peg. Stripping off my lead weight and dacron hair rigged meat, I carefully tied a size 10 barbless hook to an 8lb hook-link, grabbed my carp net, and took it with me to where the fish were basking.

As far as I could see, my only chance was to use the cover of the blackberry bush and cast beyond the fish before drawing the bread back amongst them. This I did – and all without a tangle for once – but having eased the crust gently over the surface, the King swam right past it, turned tail and cruised off into the deeper water where he disappeared from view. I was crestfallen and thought my chance had gone. Then I stupidly spooked the rest, by striking too quickly when one of the eight pounders appeared to suck at the crust. Within seconds they had all vanished.

I returned to my peg somewhat dejected and made myself a consoling cup of tea, resolving to try again later. Sure enough when I returned to the shallows after two hours, the 'boys' were back in town, and they had the King with them!

This time, I knew I would have just one chance and couldn't afford to make a mess of it again. Casting upwards and over the shoal, to a spot as close as I dare to the reeds, then drawing the baited hook back into the middle, I leaned gingerly over the bush and could just see one of the smaller fish turning towards the large chunk of bread.

But before he reached it, the King suddenly spun around with a mighty swish of his orange tail, and grabbed the bread down whole. I struck upwards. As the water erupted in an explosion of spray, the King attempted to get underneath the bush.

I tried desperately to keep the rod high so the line would clear the bush on my side.

I then slid down the steep bank on my backside to the only flat area where I could stand clear of the bush and exert some side strain and maybe turn his head. I could even land him from here, I thought.

Apart from the overhanging bush, and the reeds at the top end, there was nowhere for the King to go, and amazingly within several minutes I felt I had him under control, plodding around in front of me, hugging the bottom and releasing huge clouds of mud. With sinking heart, it was then that I remembered my big net was still at the top of the bank!

Recalling there was another angler with his son at the other end of the pool I shouted for help. After a few minutes a man appeared behind me, high up on the bank. "Can you help me out please?" I pleaded, "my net is over there and I think I've got the biggest fish in the pool here."

Over my shoulder I saw the man move towards the bush and return holding my net. But instead of sliding down the bank to pass it to me or help land the fish – as I would have done for any fellow angler – he simply threw it, as if it was a spear.

Lacking any aerodynamic properties, the net landed with a splash, to my right, half in the water, half on the bank. With the King now almost beaten and ready for the net, I crouched down, extended my outstretched arm, and desperately tried to grab the net handle.

In that split second, I allowed the taut line to go slack, and the great golden common carp wallowing in front me, threw his huge head from side to side in a last ditch attempt to evade capture.

Suddenly, I felt the line go limp. The fish had shed the barbless hook! Distraught, I plunged the net into the water in the vain hope he might still be there, but quickly realised the *King and I* had parted company, possibly forever. Dropping my rod, I sunk to my knees with my head in my hands. The man behind said, "Unlucky mate, you nearly had him."

If only I had possessed a gun at that moment…

Chapter 13
Unlucky for some?

They say you make your own luck in this life. If that were true, I would undoubtedly be much safer if I didn't go fishing. It's just as well I am not superstitious, because there is no doubt that, with the notable exception of my son Mark's birth, the 13th day of the month has proved particularly unlucky for me over the years.

On that date I have fallen in the canal in Chester, crashed my scooter when returning from fishing, fallen down the bank and damaged knee ligaments, and in 1998, came as close as I ever have to meeting my maker.

While that is a story for later in this book, it serves to underline the point that far from being the sedentary pastime my wife suggests, fishing is actually as dangerous as say, hang-gliding or climbing. Indeed, every year sea anglers are sadly lost from boats and rocks, while inland there are tragedies involving drowning or carbon poles touching power cables plus numerous non-life-threatening accidents.

However, no fishing related tragedy has ever moved me like the murder of two 11-year-olds, Robert Gee and Paul Barker. They were viciously attacked while fishing a pond alongside a motorway in Eastham on the Wirral, a few years back, not a hundred yards from the housing estate where they lived.

That shocking murder, which made national headlines, hit my fishing companion, Garry Doolan, particularly badly, as he knew both Robert Gee, and his parents well as they lived in the same avenue, and often chatted about fishing over the garden fence. The man convicted of their murder, Steven Heaney, also lived near the estate.

When I think back to the days Ian Courtney and I enjoyed on similar ponds, at the same age, it puts my supposed bad luck in its true perspective, and sends a shudder down my spine...

Even though I now carry out a mental risk assessment every time I arrive on the bankside, and wear my lifejacket if I suspect the water is deep, I still manage to have more than my share of accidents, often from the most innocuous of situations.

A session fishing for carp on Woodlands pool at the Burton Mere complex, almost 10 years ago, was typical. I had set my stall to fish two lines of attack, one to the edge of the island in front of me, and the other under an overhanging tree to my right, where I had seen tell-tale swirls in the margin.

With only a small gap in the trees to effect a cast to the edge of the island, I concentrated all my efforts on avoiding a tangle with the offending branches. To this end, I even left my hooklength off and practised several times to try and establish the correct weight of cast.

At last satisfied that I could reach the corner of the island without hindrance, I tied on my hooklength and a hair rigged strawberry-flavoured boillie. To my amazement, the lead plopped into the lake exactly where I intended.

Either I'm getting better or I'm on a lucky streak, I thought. The swim to my right would be a piece of cake by comparison. Swinging the 1½oz lead back and forth a few times, like a pendulum, I finally cast underarm towards the reed-fringed margin beneath the overhanging tree; but instead of the anticipated splash as the rig hit the water, there was silence. I peered into the greenery.

The whole rig was wrapped around one of the branches. I decided to see if I could yank it free, but only succeeded in wedging the exposed size 12 hook further into the bark.

As far as I could see I had a straight choice. Either pull for a break – with all the inherent dangers that carries – or climb the tree and see if I could separate the hook from the bark. Now, I am far too heavy to scramble up trees, but this looked eminently feasible, as the trunk split into a 'V' shape with several off-shoot branches which could provide footholds.

Besides, I could see my lead and rig, which appeared to be within easy reach. Carefully selecting each foothold, I gingerly ascended the trunk until I was level with my tangled rig. Unfortunately, it was just a little further from my fingertips than I had calculated. Squeezing my body through the branches, I put my considerable weight against the opposing angle of the 'V' shaped trunk, grabbed the lead in my hand and was trying to unravel the hook length when there was a shuddering creak beneath me.

Seconds later, the 'V' section of the tree against which I was leaning, snapped cleanly, like the wishbone of a turkey, crashing into the water below and propelling me head first with it.

Though the foliage cushioned my fall into the lake it was nevertheless a shock to the system as the water was still quite cold, despite the recent arrival of May. As the water saturated my padded, and supposedly water-proof, one-piece suit, I was conscious of losing my spectacles and cap as the lake slowly absorbed me into its dark and secret world until I was totally submerged.

This time, however, I had the good sense to keep my eyes and mouth shut. Fortunately, in the darkness my hand felt something solid and I quickly reached the conclusion there was no real depth and tried to right myself, which proved particularly intractable as moon boots full of trapped air tend to act like buoys and float to the surface!

Eventually, I righted myself and stood up in about 3ft 6ins of water to a round of ironic cheers from other anglers, and wondered how in God's name I was going to find my spectacles. After five minutes of rooting around on the bottom I was on the point of giving up when the optonic on my island line screamed off. Ploughing through the water to my peg, I grabbed the rod from its rests and snapped shut the free-running spool to put the brakes on the running fish.

Standing in water up to my waist, my cheap but functional Shakespeare carp rod lurched into a healthy bend as I cranked the reel to gain some line on what was clearly a good carp. I have always found the faster the fish tears off on its initial run the smaller it is likely to be when landed, but this was slow and ponderous indicating a bigger specimen.

Having established control, the carp circled endlessly in front of me hugging the lake bottom, seemingly unprepared to reveal itself. But 15lbs main line, a dacron hook link and a 2¼lbs test curve rod does give you a distinct advantage, and, within five minutes, a carp of more than 10lbs was gulping air and accepting the battle was over.

I reached onto the bank and grabbed the handle of my huge carp net. Sinking it deep into the water until it touched bottom, I drew it slowly and methodically upwards so the net swallowed up the fettered and defeated fish.

"You stuffy bugger." shouted someone on the other side of the lake. I grinned. Within seconds I had to agree with him.

Unravelling the net to reveal a pristine, fully scaled mirror carp, which tipped my spring balance at 11½lbs, I was astounded to serendipitously find my gold-rimmed reading spectacles, covered in mud, lying in the bottom of the net!

I can only deduce I must actually have kicked them towards my peg as I waded from where I fell in, to the position I played the fish. Mr 'Unlucky' one minute, Mr 'Stuffy' the next!

Though I enjoyed quite a few night sessions under the stars during my carp fishing days – some of them shared with my son Mark – I never felt the need to purchase a specialist Bivvy and all the accoutrements the modern carp angler regards as essential.

Indeed, it never fails to amuse me when I see someone dressed in full camouflage, like a Royal Marine commando, launching his rigs fully 80 yards. At that range he could have worn a pink chiffon sarong, navvy boots and a flying helmet without the merest prospect of spooking his quarry!

While I can almost forgive the carp angling fraternity their preoccupation with technical gizmos like optonics, anti-eject hooks, and even bait boats, I find myself appalled by the increasing use of alcohol and soft drugs to complement overnight sessions in a bivvy.

While I will admit to enjoying a social drink after fishing, I cannot understand those who either smoke cannabis or consume so much beer they spoil everyone else's enjoyment and render themselves incapable of responding to a run in the middle of the night.

I particularly remember the antics of two 'carpies'

from West Bromwich I met at Docklow Pools several years ago. Nicknamed 'Derek and Clive' after Peter Cooke and Dudley Moore's famous alter egos, they advised me to, "Get a pop up bivvay so yow can 'ave a drink while yow fish."

Proudly showing off the inside of their green nylon shelter, they had more cans of beer than you would find in a branch of Threshers.

Fishing was merely a sideline to the more serious business of getting blind drunk, and the end result was several takes by fish that went unchecked until it was too late and the fish was snagged.

Of course, night fishing at long range using bolt rigs and boillies is not a prerequisite for catching big carp. While carp anglers sleep soundly in their bivvies, the carp are often no more than inches from the bank, mopping up everything that fell out of their spods and catapults earlier.

Some six years ago, long after I had stopped specifically targeting the species, I caught my biggest ever carp, a 15lbs mirror, at Brookside near Warrington, on a match rod and 4lbs line to a 2lbs hook link with a 16 hook baited with a humble worm. The fish was grubbing around in the late afternoon, right alongside the platform upon which I was seated, when I dropped my bait in front of its nose. Had I known how big it was though, I might just have scaled up my hook link!

Apart from beating my own personal best by 8oz, what gave me more pleasure was the fact it was caught under the noses of three one method carp anglers with the usual multiple rod set ups, who hadn't had a run between them in two days.

As I pointed out in the previous chapter, there are very few venues in the north west that hold carp in excess of 30lbs. One of them is the River Weaver, which wends its way northwards through the Cheshire countryside from Nantwich to Northwich, where it becomes canalised and navigable, before eventually discharging into the Mersey near Runcorn.

Having seen photographs of Weaver carp up to 38lbs, and heard stories of even bigger specimens, it was natural that along with Garry, and later my friend Chris McGuinness, I should target the most prolific stretch, known as the Boatyard, near Northwich. Like those broad French or Belgian canals, the Weaver Navigation was around 20ft deep down the middle and punctuated by locks throughout its length. Halfway between Hunts Lock and the blue bridge at Hartford, a boatyard was enclosed by the old river arm on one side and the canalised section on the other.

With little flow, both the 'arm', and the stretch alongside the boatyard, were home (and still are) to some huge carp of every species, including crucians.

On one side there was a busy towpath but on the other boats ranging from coal steamers to pleasure cruisers were moored, affording the carp plenty of cover as they patrolled up and down the stretch in search of food.

In the opinion of the posse of carp anglers encamped along the towpath, the way to locate the better fish was to cast as close as possible to the hull of the moored boats. That was easy for them to say. They hadn't seen my casting.

Selecting a swim opposite a large and rusting coal barge, one of several moored on the boatyard side, I baited my inside line with hair rigged luncheon meat but used a small squid and shrimp boillie buried inside a PVA bag full of trout pellets on the long line. According to my fishing diary, the tactic resulted in a stunningly beautiful golden common carp in pristine condition, which weighed 9lbs. I recall the fish tried to wrap my line around the boat rudder before I finally slipped the net under it.

Something my log didn't say is that in order to reach the 'hot' spot, it was necessary to overcast my lead so it bounced off the steel hull of the barge and into the water alongside. Clearly, you couldn't do this while there was anyone on board, or working in the yard nearby, as the metallic clang reverberated around the yard, but obviously the boat owners were getting wise to the tactic and retribution was never far away. Some owners had apparently fixed barbed wire 'skirts' below water level.

The next time, coincidentally August 13th, I went to the Boatyard on the Weaver, the length was occupied by a number of expensive looking pleasure cruisers, but of greater concern to me was that the trees behind had all grown considerably and their foliage would, I concluded, hamper accurate casting. There was also a good deal more rowing activity with dozens of budding Sir Steven Redgraves practising throughout the length.

I set up my usual approach, but had grave difficulty side casting anywhere near the moored cruisers. Each cast dropped 10 yards short, so I unclipped the line, paying out what I estimated to be some 24ft of line – twice the length of my rod, plus a bit more – from the spool and clipped up again. That, I told myself, would drop the rig just short of the boat.

Taking aim, I launched the rig with a sideways lob, confident there would be a splash a few feet from the hull of the cruiser. Instead, to my amazement, the lead flew straight through an open cabin window, leaving me tethered to something inside! If I had tried to do that, I would still have been there to this day. I was mortified. "That has to be your most accurate cast ever," laughed Garry, adding, "weight wise, I'd say that's got to be a new personal best too!"

In desperation, I tugged for a break, without success, although the cruiser seemed to move against its moorings. Then I saw what I figured could be my saviour – a four man scull heading towards me, blades thrashing the river surface rhythmically, accompanied by shouts of "full pressure, full pressure" from the diminutive cox.

Quickly, I lowered my line to the surface as they glided by and was, for once, extremely grateful for the whiplash-like twang of broken nylon that indicated I had at last become separated from my potential nemesis. The cox however clearly thought he'd been shot at and was still screaming like a banshee when his boat shuddered to a halt half a mile up river!

On the basis I didn't fancy having an argument with him or explaining to the owner of the cruiser why there was a large lead and hook buried in his galley table, we cowardly decided to move pegs. As we gathered up our gear, Garry pointed at the cruiser and chuckled, "Have you seen what it's called? My eyes moved to the bow. In gold letters it said *'Lucky Star'*."

It probably was until I came along on the 13th of the month.

Chapter 14
Stupid bloody cow!

It is a matter of regret that Mark never took to fishing as he grew into adulthood. While he accompanied me when he was younger – and caught well on occasions – the sport never offered enough physical challenge, or raw excitement, to 'hook him' for life.

From eight years old onwards, he was far more interested in playing football, and was somewhat better at it than I ever was. Thus, when he reached the age when he could play competitive junior football, Sundays during the winter months were spent watching and supporting him, and his team, Pensby Falcons. But during the summer months we got plenty of fishing in and spent many an enjoyable day together at Hickory Hollow. While I was prepared to wait for the bigger carp, Mark, lacking the same degree of patience, preferred to fish for the more prolific rudd and crucian carp. Like father, like son, there were often plenty of tangles to sort out though!

One of the downsides of Hickory was that there were no proper toilets on site, and little cover where one could avail oneself of the natural flora and fauna without being in the view of other anglers, or the neighbouring houses whose back gardens overlooked the lakes. If you were taken short, however, it was only a few hundred yards walk out of the car park, around a small industrial estate to a large pub, which seemed to be open from lunch hour onwards. In all the times I had been to Hickory, thankfully, I had never found it necessary to take advantage of that facility.

On the one occasion I did, typically, I found the pub closed and boarded up for renovation.

That desperate urge for a toilet, around tea-time, also put me in a quandary – every parent's nightmare. Should I take Mark with me, or leave him at the fishery with the tackle? While my first instinct was to take him along to the pub, I accepted the offer of 'custody' from the angler on the next peg, after he revealed he was an off-duty policeman and showed me his warrant card.

Generally, I have always found the family of angling to be honest, and supportive of each other, and I considered I couldn't do much better than leave Mark in the care of a 'Bobby'. Having sorted that out, I bowed to my stomach gripes and headed to the pub, only to find it surrounded by hoardings and a full skip. What now, I thought? There was nowhere else nearby, and my need was getting greater by the minute.

I walked briskly back towards the fishery car park with the intention of driving somewhere, when I passed the entrance to what appeared to be a deserted industrial estate consisting of several units, only a couple of which, I noted, seemed to have tenants.

For a moment I stood and deliberated. It was quiet, almost comatose, and I was desperate. Needs must, I thought. I looked around me and concluded the population of Whitchurch must have been engrossed in the *Six o'clock News*. I walked around the estate until I found a quiet corner, away from the gaze of the nearby houses, commandeering a damp newspaper and a piece of cardboard from an overflowing skip en route. Placing the cardboard beneath me, I undid my trousers and crouched down. It was at that point that I was conscious

136

of the low drone of an electric motor. I looked around me but could not see anything that might generate such a noise.

I was just at the point of putting the Sun newspaper to the use to which it is best suited when out of the corner of my eye I saw something move on the roof of the building opposite – a CCTV camera! As I watched the camera stir, its lens revolving as if focusing its eye, it dawned on me that my private moment was being observed, and possibly recorded, by persons unknown, maybe miles away.

Embarrassing as it might be, there was not a lot I could do about it at that moment, other than pull down the peak of my cap and wave!

Taking care to deposit the newspaper and cardboard back in the skip where I had found them, I sauntered, rather sheepishly, out of the industrial estate, my every move shadowed by the spying eye of the CCTV camera. Maybe they don't get that many thrills in Whitchurch, I thought.

Returning to Mark and my evening's fishing, I neglectfully forgot to tell the policeman where I eventually found relief, but thanked him profusely for looking after my precious son.

It was an incident I had totally forgotten about until about two years ago when idly flicking through the various satellite TV channels I chanced upon a programme ingeniously titled *Caught on CCTV*. As I watched, the presenter was telling viewers about a couple caught one night clearly having sex, standing up, in a shop doorway in Newcastle, who even had the cheek to wave to the prying camera.

What a pair of exhibitionists, I mused. But my jaw dropped at the next item as the presenter prattled, "and this man decided a deserted Shropshire industrial estate was just the place to relieve himself…"

There I am, in all my glory, crouched down alongside some roller shutter doors with my trousers by my ankles, waving inanely at the camera! Thankfully, my face was all fuzzy so no one, other than me, would ever have known who it was. But now you all know!

Towards the mid-nineties, I was becoming a little disillusioned with what I would loosely call the 'carp scene' and their belief that only size matters. I found that to admit one hadn't caught a 20 was to invite derision and some of the lobotomy sufferers I found myself fishing alongside clearly did not share my belief that to truly appreciate the joy of fishing, one must respect not only the fish and the environment, but fellow anglers. While there are a good deal of very dedicated, and respectful, carp anglers out there, sadly there is a minority who have no concept of bankside etiquette or angling ethics. I decided to leave them to it.

Thankfully, a chance conversation en route to Wembley with a chap in his late twenties named Mark Jones, who was the future son-in-law of one of my closest friends, Charlie Hynes, opened the door to a return to all round coarse fishing at club level.

Talking fishing during the coach journey, it transpired Jonesy was a member of a relatively exclusive local angling club, which had so few members, it was more like a syndicate.

When he offered to take me to his club waters as a guest, I jumped at the opportunity, and was delighted by the fishing, the beauty of the waters, and most importantly, the friendliness of the members I met, both on the bank, and at a social gathering a few weeks later.

It was sometime however before my application

was accepted, but that did not preclude me from fishing elsewhere in the meantime with Jonesy, and another guy I met at the social, Chris McGuinness. Chris and I hit it off immediately and within weeks had become regular fishing companions – it was just like the old days with Ian and co.

Then in his late twenties, Chris was, and still is, a very good angler, who could plonk a feeder in the same spot 50 yards away, nine times out of ten. A useful exponent of the pole, he also encouraged me to invest in an 11 metre version – one of the best moves I ever made.

But it wasn't long before he became acutely aware of my shortcomings and perennial bad luck. One balmy summer's day we went to Cheshire Fishing near Tattenhall, a large commercial complex of coarse and fly-fishing pools set beneath the Peckforton Hills.

Though there were plenty of big carp in the venue – some of which showed to floating crust in the heat of the mid-day sun – I was quite enjoying myself bagging up on quality crucians, roach and tench which responded well to corn and caster. Unfortunately, I was also being plagued by crayfish and they don't half nip – but not as bad as insects!

Trying to keep up my fluid intake, I opened a can of Pepsi, took a sip and placed it in the side tray of my Shakespeare seat box as I struck into a decent tench. Holding my pole upwards to allow the elastic to do its job, I netted a specimen of maybe 3lbs. After releasing the fish, I reached for my drink and took another swig.

With a yell that attracted the attention of just about everybody else on the complex, I jumped up holding my mouth, and saw something zip across in front of my eyes. My lips and gums felt as if they were on fire. "What in Christ's name is up with you?" shouted Chris.

I told him I thought a wasp or bee had just stung me in the mouth.

Within minutes, my left cheek and lips had swollen up and reddened, while my eye had almost closed. "Jesus, you look like the Elephant Man," said Chris, laughing. The pain, though, was excruciating, and within half-an-hour I had decided to pack up and head for the nearest hospital. "That could happen to anyone," observed Chris, adding, "You were just unlucky."

A couple of weeks later I think Chris realised there was more too it than just bad luck. We went to Harthill, but not the lower lake where I had once lost a huge carp I called the 'King'. Since my last visit the owner had removed the trout from the top lake and transformed it into a mixed coarse fishery of some note containing huge tench, big roach and wild carp. Hedging my bets, I floatfished close in on one line and fixed a running lead on my carp rod, casting as near to the island as I could manage, on the other, relying on my optonic (which I later left in the grass and never saw again) to warn me of any action.

Using 8lbs main line tied to a small swivel, a running lead, and a 6lbs hook-link with a size 14 barbless hook baited with two pieces of corn, I was hopeful that one of the big tench or wild carp might show interest, and sure enough mid-way through the day I did get a screaming take. Having peeled maybe 30 yards of line from my reel I decided the time had come to put the brakes on and recover some line. Dipping the rod tip beneath the water and applying steady side pressure, I brought the fish – presumably a good 'wildie' – to within 10 yards of me when it suddenly took fright again and bolted smashing my hook-link.

Sickened by the loss, I set about tying on a new eyed

hook. Using a half-tucked blood knot to secure it to the long hook-link, I brushed the hook against my tongue to apply some spittle to dampen the knot, before tightening and trimming it.

Unfortunately for me, at that very moment the lead slipped from between my knees, tightening the line and thrusting the hook point into my tongue! With the hook impaled in my tongue, I called to Chris for help in what could best be described as a low monotone grunt and waved my arms like a village idiot!

When he finally stopped laughing at my predicament, he delicately eased the hook out of my tongue and handed me a clean towel to bite on to stop the bleeding.

Boy, was I glad I use barbless hooks exclusively these days. "You're different class. We need someone like you in the club purely for the entertainment value," was Chris's backhand complement. And so it was that I was accepted into the bosom of the angling club, amongst some of the friendliest people you could wish to meet – a world apart from my previous experience of club angling.

That summer Maria, Mark and I (our daughter was abroad with a friend) took a week's holiday in the south east of England, with the intention of combining visits for Mark to the wildlife park at Howletts near Canterbury, and Colchester Zoo with sight-seeing in Kent and East Anglia. While Maria took Mark to the zoos, yours truly sneaked off with his fishing tackle to nearby venues, which I had carefully pre-selected. Near Canterbury, I fished Chilham match lake; a giant doughnut shaped, man made lake almost universally 14 metres wide. Initially, I struggled until helped out by some local kids who advised me to fish down the track with bread. Finally, I netted several small carp, crucians, and roach to make my short visit worthwhile.

While I later had an early morning session – and blanked – on the beautiful, but weedy, Taverham Mills lake near Norwich, an unscheduled detour, while driving northwards towards Norfolk, was to prove the setting for yet another of my seemingly endless unusual fishing experiences.

Seeing a sign for Flatford Mill, I could not resist the temptation to see the inspiration for John Constable's famous painting of 1817. 'Constable Country' did not disappoint, and after booking ourselves into a B&B in the village of East Bergholt, where the great artist was born, we wandered down to the picturesque old mill that straddles the narrow and sluggish River Stour. It has hardly changed in 200 years.

In the gift shop at Flatford, I was delighted to discover a two-mile section of this idyllic river was fishable on a day ticket, and decided to spend much of the following day, Sunday, on the stretch.

Armed with corn, meat, bread and groundbait plus some week-old maggots, I lugged my tackle across a wrought iron footbridge, but was halted in my tracks halfway over by an amazing sight. In gin clear water beneath the bridge was a big shoal of huge bream just sitting in the current, while on the other side, resting their bellies on the shale bottom, were several handsome barbel. Unfortunately, there was a sign both sides saying 'No Fishing' which no doubt explains their presence at that location.

Selecting a likely spot on the deserted river, opposite a lush meadow full of grazing cows, I sat down and set up my Avon rod, drinking in the most quintessential of English landscapes, and listening to the peel of bells from the historic village church I could see in the distance.

Starting with legered double maggot, I caught one plump roach and a couple of nuisance eels, before switching to a large cube of luncheon meat for the chub and barbel, which I suspected might be near a sunken tree on the far side. Just then I noticed a rather ungainly cow gingerly trying to negotiate the steeply sloping bank opposite me, to drink from the river. Attempting to slide down on her haunches she finally lost her balance, and with a huge splash, fell headfirst into the river right in front of me. Now, I never knew cows could swim, but rest assured they can.

Three times 'Ermintrude' tried to clamber out at the spot she fell in, but each time the gradient and muddy bank defeated her, and she sank back into the river. This is ridiculous I thought. Two bloody miles of river and a cow has to fall in my swim.

A middle-aged woman walking a dog stopped behind me to watch the spectacle.

After five minutes busily wrecking the fishing potential of my swim by swimming backwards and forwards along the stretch, 'Ermintrude', by now clearly exhausted, finally found a flatter section of bank, about 50 yards upstream and staggered out of the river. In that lovely East Anglian drawl the dog owner leaned over and enquired, "ave yew 'ad anythin?"

"Yes," I replied, "A two ton Friesian, but I threw it back 'cos it wouldn't fit in my keepnet." She obviously didn't appreciate my humour and walked off in a huff.

"Stupid bloody cow," I muttered, under my breath.

Chapter 15
A swan song of revenge

For reasons not unconnected to the imposition of a £5 fine during my teenage years, I had not fished the mighty River Severn for over 25 years when Chris suggested a trip to a section near Shrewsbury, renowned for barbel fishing.

While Chris, as a civil servant, enjoyed a cheap annual licence, I had to buy a £3 day ticket, in advance, from the local tackle shop, but figured it was worth the trouble, as I had never caught a barbel in all my years of fishing. This was one deficiency I was determined to rectify, but as usual, my quest would not be without incident...

While the Severn is undoubtedly one of the country's premier river fisheries, reaching the best swims can be both tortuous and physically demanding.

Negotiating gates and stiles laden down with tackle and upwards of eight pints of hemp, battling through barley fields, and slithering down steep and muddy banks, often make fishing this river prohibitive for all but the fittest and most determined of anglers.

Certainly, on the first occasion Chris and I hiked the mile-and-a-half from the car park to our pegs with all our gear I was shattered.

Taking Chris's advise, I set up two rods with feeders packed with hemp and caster, baiting the hook, alternately with double maggot, corn or curried meat cubes.

Having first established the water right in front of me was fairly shallow, I positioned my box on a convenient shelf halfway down the steeply sloping bank, and balanced the two rods on a single quiver rest in front of me, with the white painted tips pointing skywards to keep the line off the surface.

Despite the fact I was apparently sitting on a known barbel haunt, all I had to show for my efforts was a few dace, gudgeon and perch; but Chris was rewarded for his persistence with a sleek fish of 5½lbs.

It must have been early afternoon when the head of the plastic quiver rest suddenly rotated 180 degrees, propelling the rods forwards towards the river. Instinctively, I tried to grab them before they fell, but only succeeded in losing my balance and diving head-first from my perch, into the water below.

While the river, low after a dry summer but chilled by the first frosts of October, may only have been a foot or so deep down the edge, it was more than enough to soak me from the waist downwards.

Worse still, my spectacles were seemingly swept downstream by the current. Despite groping around I failed to find them this time.

Listening to a Liverpool v Manchester United match commentary in his earphones, Chris was totally oblivious to my aquatic exploration on the next peg, and was at first amused and then mortified, when I ploughed through the water, utterly sodden, to tell him what had happened. "You could have been swept away and I wouldn't have known," he said with genuine concern.

Thankfully, the rods were undamaged, and even though my trousers and underwear were soaked, I continued to fish for the rest of the day. Later that afternoon, our club chairman, Eddie Johnson, turned up on the same stretch and after hearing my tale of woe, said, "well, that's your nickname sorted then. I think we shall call you *'wet suit'*.

It is a tag that has stuck with me ever since.

Unfortunately, that wasn't the end of the day's disasters. On our return journey to the car, we discovered the farmer had released two angry looking bulls into one of the fields we had to pass through.

While I was confident they wouldn't attack unless provoked, Chris was less convinced and literally ran across the field, carrying all his gear. I adopted a more pedestrian, but nevertheless cautious approach, skirting the bankside undergrowth, which I reasoned could provide a degree of protection to hide in should one of the animals decide to charge.

Though they stalked us, snorting and tossing their heads from side to side menacingly as if looking for the merest hint of fear to justify a pre-emptive strike, neither charged, and we were both able to make the stile safely.

Chris said he was sweating that much his clothing was nearly as damp as mine!

There was worse to come when we got back to my car. On arrival that morning, Chris had taken a three-pint bait container, half full of unwanted 'pinkies', out of his box to reduce the load, placing it in the corner of my boot.

When I opened the tailgate to pack away the gear, at least half the contents had escaped through the lid and were all over the load space – and beyond.

While Chris and I did our best to scoop them up, hundreds had invaded the front of the car and were in every nook and cranny – from under the floor mats to the CD rack.

Though I did another sweep when I got home, within three weeks, the inside of the car was full of small flies. It was so bad that each morning I had to open both doors to evacuate the overnight hatch before I could drive off! Maria was not amused.

I finally caught my first barbel the following summer, a wonderful specimen weighing 7lbs 2ozs, and enjoyed several other successful sessions – the best being when Chris and I shared 15 barbel to 6½lbs – along the same stretch.

Given my penchant for falling in, Chris thereafter chose swims that could accommodate us both, fishing side by side. Not only did this arrangement ensure I didn't come to any harm, it meant we were in a position to help each other landing fish.

Anyone who has ever fished with two rods will confirm that Sod's Law dictates that sooner or later you will get a big fish on both lines, at the same time.

One day, in July 1996, Chris was busy battling with a large barbel that was using the strong current to its advantage, when the tip of his other rod banged around.

"Get that one for me will you?" asked Chris. Trying desperately not to foul his line I somehow managed to steer a tench of just under 5lbs to the net. Minutes later, Chris netted an 8lbs barbel with a hunchback.

I argued the tench represented a new personal best for me, but Chris maintained it didn't count because I caught it on *his* rod and it wasn't indigenous to the river anyway. I responded by reminding him barbel were introduced in the 1950s!

Later in the day, I had my own stroke of luck for a change, twice breaking my personal best for a barbel; firstly with one of 7lbs 6ozs, and then a magnificent specimen of 8lbs 10ozs, which fought like a tiger for fully ten minutes. I also caught a best ever chub weighing 4½lbs.

While I delight in catching virtually every species of coarse fish – with the exception of small skimmers – the magnificent and sleek fighting machine that is the barbel remains a particular favourite, and to a degree, I can understand why certain anglers target them above other species.

Having enjoyed a red-letter day with three new PBs, you might think I had used up all my luck, but my biggest break came late that afternoon.

Since my earlier indiscretion, I have always made sure I carried a valid Environmental Agency Licence, but I will admit to having taken the occasional liberty with club owned waters – and that day was one of them.

When my pre-paid day ticket failed to materialise in the post, rather than drop out, I took a late, and almost fatal, decision to borrow Jonesy's card for the stretch, and present that to the local water bailiff if challenged.

What I hadn't bargained for was the club bailiff *and* the Environmental Agency bailiff arriving together! As they slid down the bank to the large double swim where Chris and I were fishing, I was overcome by a dreadful sense of *deja vu*.

Because there were two of us on the peg, the EA man came to me first, and of course, I was able to show him a valid licence in my own name, while the local bailiff inspected Chris' club card. They then swapped over, and when I handed over a club card in the name of 'Mark Jones' the local bailiff seemed quite satisfied, and we engaged in some cheery dialogue about the fish – including the rogue tench – we had caught, before they headed off across the field.

I let out a huge sigh of relief. "Christ, that was close," I said. For the next 10 minutes I kept peering over the precipice of the bank, fully expecting them to turn tail once they realised there was a discrepancy with the names they had been given. Thankfully, they never did, but it taught me a valuable lesson. I don't take chances any more.

That summer, Chris and I enjoyed the first of three 'boys only' annual fishing holidays at Docklow pools near Leominster in Herefordshire. Having been dragged along to Docklow the previous year, Chris's wife was content to let him go with me instead, while Maria was probably glad to see the back of me for a week.

Hidden away in a beautiful valley, Docklow is a 100 acre complex with eight mature pools, accommodation in stone cottages, and even its own pub and tackle shop, all run by Josie and Mike Bozward. He had sunk all his redundancy money from British Leyland into creating it over 25 years ago.

Idyllic as it was, my first holiday there wasn't the roaring success, fishing wise, I had expected. It was, in truth, almost demoralising at times. Having said that, I started the week well with 70lbs of chub and smaller carp from the lily covered 'Mickey Mouse' pool, but found the much shallower match pool a totally different proposition. While I always try to enjoy my fishing whether I catch or not, it does irk you when you are sitting on a 'blank' while your mate, fishing in exactly the same fashion, is on his way to the magical ton just a couple of pegs away.

My day started badly and fell away thereafter. While I had an island rich in trees with overhanging branches directly in front of me, Chris was able to cast further out along the edge of the island and was regularly taking carp to about 7lbs off the surface on dog biscuit. Using a heavy controller to reach the island, my first cast only succeeded in finding the overhanging tree branches, and after five minutes of tugging, I lost the whole set up. Having decided a loaded waggler would be lighter, and be less likely to spook the fish, I scattered several pouches of dog biscuit on the surface, and when the carp were feeding confidently, cast my biscuit hookbait beyond the floaters, so that I could gently draw it back amongst them.

When it works there is no doubt this technique can provide thrilling sport, but when it doesn't, and the fish are cagey, there is nothing more frustrating.

Despite the element of competition for the 'freebies', the carp and chub in my swim simply mopped up every floating biscuit but always ignored the spongy one that had my hook buried in, or glued to it.

In contrast, Chris had the fish in a frenzy two pegs away and ended the day with over 100lbs. Having lost three good carp, my catch consisted of two chub and a bream before I eventually conceded defeat and moved pegs.

Not only is Chris a good angler, he is, by his own admission, a lucky one too. Seeing a carp apparently towing a huge controller float across the surface, Chris cast beyond it and carefully drew his own float and hook across the path of the loose float, hoping, somewhat forlornly, to snag the line and release the tethered fish from his ordeal. To my amazement, he managed to thread his hook through the bottom ring of the huge surface float, bringing both that and the attached six-pound carp to the net.

The only thing I could hook consistently on the surface was ducks. I think my tally for the week almost exceeded that for carp. I even managed to reverse over one in the car park.

Though I fell in love with Docklow, and in particular the beautiful 'Micky Mouse' and 'Moby Dick' pools, which were surrounded by mature oaks, cedars, and weeping willows, it wasn't because I enjoyed outstanding success there. Quite the contrary.

It was the place's unpredictability that enchanted, as well as frustrated, me.

Asking Mike, the owner, one day where the big carp could be found, he recommended we follow the wind into the top corner of 'Moby Dick', at the opposite end to the car park, where all the day ticket summer anglers fall out of their cars to fish for crucians and roach.

Chris and I fished that top corner for two days without getting anything bigger than 10lbs, yet we heard later someone who admitted he fished a couple of times a year when the sun shone, caught a 21lb carp in 18 inches of water a few yards from his parked car!

"I think we should pack it in, and take up golf," said Chris.

The final insult was yet to come, though. On our last day, Chris and I fished on different lakes, but were actually sitting virtually back to back. While Chris fished 'Moby Dick', I fished a swim on 'Micky Mouse' known as 'the boards' because the cruising carp patrolled the margins, brushing their backs against the wooden boards.

The favoured technique was to sit well back and lay a trap with plenty of corn by the boards and then fish a huge lump of meat over it, utilising rod and strong line, rather than pole.

There are few aspects of angling more exciting than margin fishing. When you can actually see the dark shadows and tail swirls as fish arrive in your swim, the sense of anticipation is ever more acute.

With my trap set, all I had to do was to wait, but I hadn't bargained for the unwelcome curiosity of the resident swans, who scrutinised me closely as I emptied three tins of sweetcorn into 18 inches of water down the edge.

Three times the pair tried to move in on the corn only to be thwarted by a discouraging wave of my landing net handle. Much hissing followed before they reluctantly withdrew, gracefully gliding off up the lake to annoy someone else. While they were away, I caught several reasonable carp and a barbel.

Around six o'clock I ambled up to the cottage to make something to eat, having re-baited the swim before I left. But when I returned I could see the swans, their heads under the water, busy mopping up all the corn! Once again, a lot of arm waving on my part brought about a begrudging, hissing, retreat.

Chris and I fished until darkness descended, but as usual, I had already packed up when Chris asked me to help land his final fish of the session. When I returned for my gear, one of the swans was perched defiantly on top of my Rive seat-box.

As I approached, the swan lifted its tail feathers, flapped its wings a couple of times, and then emptied its bowels all over my seat-box before jumping back into the water with a victorious squawk!

"Now, *that's* what you call revenge!" said Chris, laughing.

Chapter 16
Bishop's sore pole shock

If he had so chosen, there is no doubt John Aldridge could have been a match winner on the bank, instead of the football field. Known to the football world simply as 'Aldo', the Republic of Ireland goalscoring hero has that mean competitive streak that all professional sportsmen must have if they want to succeed. Whether in the penalty box sniffing out chances, or sitting beside a lake after carp, being a winner is all-important.

In my capacity as programme editor to Tranmere Rovers, I first met John in 1990 when he signed for the newly promoted club from Real Sociedad. Even though we spoke regularly, it wasn't until I saw a magazine article showing John holding an Irish pike, that I realised we had something, other than football, in common.

These days there seems to be an increasing number of high profile footballers who have turned their back on the traditional footballers' pastime, golf, in favour of the peace and quiet of fishing. David Seaman, Lee Bowyer, and Paul Gascoigne are three who spring readily to mind.

Talking to John, I quickly learned how passionate he is about fishing, and how his late father, Bill, had introduced him to the sport as a young boy.

Ever since then, wherever his career has taken him, his fishing tackle has gone too.

While Newport was not the best location for coarse fishing, his years at Oxford proved particularly fruitful with an abundance of big fish lakes on his doorstep.

John even fished when he was out in Spain, though the lakes and rivers proved challengingly different to what he was used to.

The biggest problem for John, and other high profile footballers is finding the solitude and privacy they crave. One day, John, Garry and I went to Hickory Hollow mid-week during school term, yet within hours of our arrival his concentration was regularly disturbed by well-meaning teenagers, and adults, seeking autographs, photographs, and a chat about football.

Though John was never less than courteous and obliging with every request, I felt for him, and resolved to try and find a remote, and more private, venue that we could fish content in the knowledge he would not be disturbed.

Watching John's casting, presentation and methodical feeding, there is no doubt in my mind that if had been able to devote more time to his fishing over the years he could have become as successful an angler as he was a professional footballer – though clearly not as well paid! That view was endorsed by *Tight Lines* presenter, Keith Arthur, after they fished together at Burton Mere for a Sky TV feature. As I told John, "the only thing that spoilt your image was that white reclining patio chair. For a minute, I thought I was watching a gardening programme!"

Eventually, I found the perfect venue for John to fish, near Prestatyn in north Wales. Fishable only by appointment, and with a relatively high cost day ticket, the venue offered both seclusion and exclusivity on two idyllic and tranquil estate lakes, set in the grounds of an old Castle. Though there are carp to 32lbs in the lakes – we watched several huge specimens cruising in the shallows – typically, John and I couldn't catch one.

But we did fill our keepnets with maybe 50lbs apiece of tench, crucians and rudd. More importantly for John, we were the only people there. As a venue, it was a far cry from his first fishing trip with his dad to Sefton Park, Liverpool. According to John, he had long believed he caught his first ever fish on that occasion until Bill confessed to 'buying' it for him!

Apparently, without a bite all morning, Bill had sent young John to the shops on the pretext of buying some sweets, but while he was away 'bought' a small roach from another angler on the lake, and hooked it onto John's rod and line.

When John returned his dad pointed to the fact his float had gone under, and low and behold John wound in his first ever fish! Amazingly, Bill kept the secret for almost 30 years.

Since then, John has had a few bigger than that, and recently told me he had cracked the 'magical 20' barrier after being invited to fish a syndicate carp lake.

Commissioned to write a magazine article on John's career, and his 'passion for angling', I asked him which he would prefer, a hat-trick in a big game or a 25lbs carp? He thought for a moment, then replied, "I'll take two goals and the carp!"

Like most football people, John has an impish sense of humour, and on occasions I found myself on the end of his 'wind ups', none more so than the night of his testimonial dinner in the Liverpool Moat House Hotel.

Having been asked to design, write and produce his testimonial brochure, one of the telephone interviews I conducted was with the former Eire boss, and keen game fisherman, Jack Charlton, who was generous in his praise of John.

Now, you might recall, Jack famously got caught

without an EA licence on the opening day of the new fly fishing season, which was particularly embarrassing as he had fronted their advertising campaign to remind anglers to renew their licences!

This, of course, was not on my mind when, on the night, I asked John to introduce me to the former World Cup winner, who had been a personal hero for many years.

Taking me by the arm, John, by now fairly inebriated, guided me to Big Jack and said, "Gaffer, I'd like to introduce you to my mate Pete Bishop." As we shook hands, John cracked, "He's from the Environmental Agency, and want's to see your rod licence!"

Doubled with laughter John promptly vanished, leaving me standing uncomfortably with Jack. "Very bloody funny," he muttered in that trademark Geordie brogue. That's Aldo's name in the infamous 'black book' I thought!

Had I been able to compose my thoughts at that moment, I should have asked Jack for some tips for my forthcoming fishing holiday to Ireland.

According to John, Jack always made sure the team hotels they used in Ireland not only had a golf course and training pitch available, but some excellent lough or river fishing nearby. Apparently, he knew the Irish fishing scene inside out.

For some time, Maria had been keen on visiting Ireland, and in particular Sligo, from where her grandparents came, while I rather fancied the idea of a long overdue return to the Emerald Isle with some fishing thrown in.

Mark Lewis, our erudite club secretary, tipped me off about an excellent B&B alongside the mighty River Shannon in Roosky, which I noted, was only 40 miles from Sligo Town.

We decided to stay three nights at 'Sheena's' in Roosky, two nights at a B&B between Macroom and Cork, and two nights in Dublin. All agreed to accept our Cavalier King Charles terrier, Tessa, who travelled with us.

Shenna's large and modern house, on the banks of the Shannon, was set up with anglers in mind, and when we arrived there was a party of six 15-year-old schoolboys from Barnsley, along with their teacher, staying there.

As far as I can remember, there was no such thing as an 'activity holiday' when I was at school, though some pupils did go on exchange visits to France.

Apparently coached by Barnsley Blacks' former England star Dennis White, they were all such accomplished anglers they could have tied me in knots if I weren't so adroit at doing it myself. The lads were leaving Sheena's the day after we arrived, so that evening I enquired how they had fared, and what baits proved successful.

After directing me to an area in front of Sheena's lawn where they had been fishing, and groundbaiting all week, and handing over all their surplus bait, I set up using a heavy open-ended feeder to hold bottom on the wide and powerful Shannon.

Half an hour later I had lost three complete rigs including feeder, on the snaggy bottom, before one of the lads helpfully showed me how to tie a rig which would snap free so you would only lose the feeder itself.

There I was, a fisherman for 33 years, being 'coached' by a cheeky 15-year-old!

"Tha teacher told us if we ca' do out to help auld people we should. If tha uses this set-tup thal do 'al reet," he said with that distinctive whistle to the Yorkshire dialect that characterises people from Barnsley. He was absolutely right too, proving you are never too old to learn, even if it is from an impudent 15-year-old who thought I was past it.

Fishing just a few hours early morning and evening, I caught half a dozen slabs to 5lbs per session – at the cost of some 20 open-end feeders – plus several quality roach, while son Mark was delighted with a 5lbs pike taken on spinner.

I often wonder what happened to those lads. They are probably now fishing in the same Barnsley team as Tom Pickering and Alan Scotthorne. If only Ian Courtney and I had had the opportunity of being coached by an England international when we were 15. Mind you, we certainly enjoyed our own 'activity holidays' in Ireland without teachers around to spoil things.

Later in the week, we moved southwards to Cork where I planned to fish Inniscarra Lake– a huge reservoir created from the River Lee in the Seventies. Unfortunately, the accommodation we pre-booked near Macroom was nowhere near as welcoming as Sheena's. It was the type of place where the owner took a sharp intake of breath if you put two spoonfuls of sugar in your tea at breakfast. Mean? They even switched the grill off when they turned the bacon over!

If I found their attitude towards our dog disconcerting, I was horrified when I found four anglers from London sleeping in their van outside one afternoon, because the owner wouldn't let them in before 5pm despite the fact they had been travelling by road and boat for 22 hours.

Having been warned about sudden discharges from the reservoirs into the River Lee, I drove around the lake until I found a likely spot in a small bay where

I could ball in a 'groundbait mountain' which would attract the nomadic shoals of bream and bream/roach hybrids by the following morning. Blending a bream mix with brown crumb, corn, and casters, I carefully moulded a dozen orange-sized balls. Using a large controller float as a marker, I cast about six lengths out, to a spot in line with a white house on the opposite side of the lake, and then balled in the groundbait.

The following morning I was up at the crack of dawn, and sneaked out of 'Fawlty Towers' as Maria and Mark slept.

When I found the spot where I had intended to fish I was dumbstruck. The lake, which had been lapping the rocks around the edge the previous day, had simply vanished, and now the water's edge was some 35 yards further out!

I looked in the direction of the white house on the opposite bank and mentally counted out six rod lengths. There, in the mud, was my 'groundbait mountain', or rather, several brown 'molehills' in a loose grouping!

After establishing such wild fluctuations in level were not uncommon, I didn't bother with Inniscarra after that.

Instead, I went trout fishing on the River Bride near Cork but even that was not without incident. With my first cast the fly lodged in a tree, and with the second I hooked a sheep grazing in the field behind me.

Though the hook easily pulled through the wool I did wonder if anyone had witnessed the spectacle of a heavily built man in wellies chasing a sheep across a field!

Back in England, Chris and I discovered a prolific commercial fishery in South Cheshire, called Hampton Springs, and regularly gorged ourselves on double figure carp, green and golden tench, crucians, bream, chub, and roach, mostly using pole tactics. We even got a mention in the *Anglers Mail*.

But for some reason, we both had costly mishaps with our poles when fishing there. During one session, Chris was playing a large carp when his fifth section gave way under the pressure and split, halfway down. I watched, with grudging admiration, as he nonchalantly played out a 12lbs mirror on just four sections of pole, with number 10 elastic and 3lbs bottom, for fully 45 minutes before slipping the net under the fish.

My pole disaster at Hampton was down to my own clumsiness, though I would argue in my defence that a strong wind contributed.

Standing up to reach my rod holdall behind me, the end two, and most expensive sections, of my 11 metre pole blew off the roost, and right under my feet, as I tried to negotiate my way around my cluttered peg.

The sound of splintering carbon beneath my boots told me this was about to become one of those days when you regret getting out of bed. In attempting to regain my balance as the pole sections rolled under my feet, I only succeeded in stumbling backwards onto my side tray, snapping it clean off the Octoplus legs, and knocking all my full bait-boxes into the water and then followed them up to my thighs. Once again, Chris and Jonesy were helpless with laughter either side of me. "It was like watching a first day pupil at a lumberjack's school for log rolling," Chris said later.

After realising it would cost as much to replace the two smashed sections as it would to buy a new pole, I decided to invest almost £500 – a huge sum for me – in a new 13 metre Maver FXB2 pole.

A vast improvement on my old Maver, the new pole enabled me to reach the edge of islands previously beyond my reach, and chase fish out farther when hooked in the margins.

Coincidentally, around the time I purchased the new pole, I was conscious of some irritation on the palms of my hands, which seemed to flare up after I had been fishing and handling the pole, especially when it was wet. When the skin dried out, it often cracked open and bled. Searching for a reason for this sudden ailment, I noted that when the section joints were wet, a black dusty residue often passed onto my hands, though I recalled the same phenomena occurring with the joints on the old pole when they became worn.

I discussed the skin irritation with my father, who claimed he had experienced something similar whilst handling carbon dust in the laboratory some years before his retirement. Curious to discover if this was a common problem, I wrote to the editor of one of the weekly angling titles asking if they were aware of carbon dust from pole joints causing skin irritation to other anglers. The result of my inquiry was a sensational story in the following week's issue, ambiguously entitled *'Bishop's sore pole shock!'* claiming my hands 'broke out in bleeding sores' after buying a new Maver pole, and suggesting I must be allergic to it.

If Maver boss Phil Briscoe was infuriated with the publication – which specifically mentioned the brand name in their story – his commercial embarrassment, made clear to me during a 'phone call, was nothing compared to mine. He didn't have to put up with work-mates, club members, tackle shop owners and customers, and worst of all, courtesy of Aldo, everyone at Tranmere, shouting, "Hey Bish, how's your sore pole?"

Often using a rigid arm to mimic an erect penis,

they'd chortle, "have you tried Penicillin?" or "you should quit using the Viagra!"

For weeks I was a laughing stock, and after all that, my complaint was diagnosed to be nothing other than eczema aggravated by the dust entering the cracked skin.

Chapter 17
A tin of luncheon meat

Of the fifty-five members in our angling club, around 30 regularly fish club matches on our own waters, and various venues around Cheshire and north Wales, but no more than about eight regularly feature on the winner's roll of honour. Not surprisingly, I am not one of them.

Now, that doesn't mean I don't try. I prepare my bait and rigs with meticulous care, and have even been known to spend a day practising to get the 'feel' of an unfamiliar venue, not that its ever done me much good, because you can never simulate match conditions.

It's just that when it comes down to it, I know I am not particularly competitive, and am just there because I happen to enjoy the company and all the banter before, during, and after the event. As a matchman, I'm as much use as an ejector seat in a helicopter. If I catch, and catch well, that's a bonus.

But I recognise that for me to win, I would have to be extraordinarily lucky at the draw bag (and I possess a 'dead man's hand') while some of the better anglers in the club would need to draw duff pegs. Having said that, by some quirk of fate, I have still managed to frame on quite a few occasions. As I said in the introduction to this book, I firmly believe the route to fishing contentment is to always try your best, but acknowledge your limitations and either fish to your strengths, or learn to enjoy and appreciate, whether you catch or not.

If you look at the 'Open' match results in the angling press you will note it is always the same clique of professional, and semi-professional, match anglers who clean up the prize money each week. Talk to the average matchman, and he'll tell you his tales of woe, about the poor draws he gets, the most recent occasion he framed, or maybe even the day he won a match.

But the unpalatable truth is that most weeks he fills the pockets of the few, whilst telling himself he enjoys pitting his wits against the best. That's fair enough, but like football, those who are destined to reach the top, have usually done so by the time they are twenty-five. Alan Scotthorne and Will Raison are prime examples. Maybe that, along with the high cost of competing, explains the diminishing numbers, compared to 25 years ago, who fish 'open' matches.

Perhaps the way forward for match angling is for each competitor to be awarded a handicap, like golfers, based on their track record, which should create a more level 'playing field'. Certainly, pole length and quantity of feed should also be restricted, as it is in international competition. Mind you, I have had a 'handicap' for years – my atrocious casting and clumsiness!

Someone once said there are three stages of a sportsman's life. Great potential, never quite made it, and good committee material. Well, at 18, I realised I was, at best, 'good committee material'. At club level, though, it really doesn't matter who wins the contest, it's about a group of like-minded people who enjoy each other's company, and laughter is never far away...

About six years ago we had a member by the name of Pete Johnson, an ebullient, irrepressible character, known as 'Jono' for short. He owned his own garage, and had a seemingly endless assortment of transport available, including various cars, a motorbike, mini-bus and even a caravan.

The Transit mini bus was a god-send, enabling up to six of us, plus all our gear, to travel on outings, but it wasn't long before some heartless individual branded our transport 'the window lickers' bus', suggesting we were on a day out from the asylum.

A cruel reference, but it stuck with us for the whole season, until somebody else labelled us 'mercenaries' because we said we preferred bagging up at commercials to eking out tiny roach and gudgeon from the canal. It's all harmless banter of course, and part of the delight of club membership. Just to rile the others we had box stickers printed celebrating our 'mercenary' status! While most of our away trips are within a 50 mile radius of home, occasionally longer excursions are organised, which provide a good excuse for a weekend get together.

When we were scheduled to go to Docklow one year, around a dozen of us decided to go down the day before, fish the lakes on the Friday, and then stay overnight in B&Bs, thereby avoiding the long drive down early on the Saturday morning. Jono suggested taking his caravan as Docklow had touring pitches. However, due to business commitments, he couldn't spare the time to fish on Friday, but promised to bring his caravan down in time to provide overnight accommodation for all six of us.

We were fishing the ever-frustrating match lake at around 8.00pm when Jonesy pointed out, "there's Jono arriving." I turned to see the rear end of a white caravan disappearing between the trees en route to the area allocated to tourers.

Well, at least I've got somewhere to get my head down, I thought. About 15 minutes later Jono bounded over in his usual exuberant manner, and said he had parked up and suggested I leave my car near his, a large and distinctive Vauxhall Carlton, which he said, was alongside his caravan.

Harassed as usual by bird-life, including my old adversaries, the swans, and frustrated by the loss of a big carp in the margins to record another blank, I decided to call it a day by 8.30pm. I joined the others in the smoky and crowded bar of Docklow's own 17th century pub, appropriately named the Fisherman's Arms. Driving my car over to the caravan park, I drove past several swish caravans before I sighted Jono's big Vauxhall parked alongside a tiny, shabby caravan, propped up on bricks. It must have been 30 years old. My jaw dropped. Six of us in this heap? He had to be joking! It would be a squeeze for two people. With a sigh of resignation, I eventually locked up my car, putting the bait underneath to keep it cool, and walked up the lane to the pub.

By the time I got there the bar was packed with regular weekend visitors, holiday residents, and some 13 members of our club, all squeezed around a large oak table next to the inglenook fireplace. I immediately confronted Jono. Even though I knew he could be a prankster, this was beyond a joke. "What's your problem? We'll all fit in. Stop panicking," replied our erstwhile host. The others seemed equally sceptical. As he quaffed his pint, club chairman Eddie Johnson (no relation) added to my disquiet. "We'll need a can-opener to get you lot out in the morning. I've seen bigger tins of luncheon meat!"

Apart from the issue of the sleeping arrangements, we all enjoyed a splendid night, and were particularly entertained by one of the weekend regulars from Birmingham, a woman in her late 50s, called Jeanette, who proudly told anyone who would listen, her withered arm had "never stopped me landing 'uge cat fesh".

Despite the presence of her long-suffering husband at the bar, the more she drank, the more flirtatious she became. By the end of the night she was sitting provocatively on people's laps as the lads mischievously egged her on.

One of the last to leave around midnight, I staggered out of the Fisherman's Arms and sauntered past the lakes, in total darkness, to the caravan park, about half a mile down hill. I was grateful I had remembered my pocket torch. Arriving at my car after the others, having performed an 'Olga Korbut' summersault into a ditch en route, I found the caravan park quiet, though the lights were on and the curtains drawn in Jono's caravan.

This was going to be about as enjoyable as having a tooth pulled, I told myself as I took my sleeping bag, and Chris', from the boot of the car and knocked on the door of the 'tin of luncheon meat'.

For a few moments there was no reply, merely some shuffling and whispered tones from inside. Eventually, the door swung open on its rusty hinges. Much to my surprise, it wasn't Jono, but Jeanette, draped in a thin dressing gown that barely covered her modesty. Before I could speak she half turned to address her husband, "Oh look, it's dat big fillah from the pub, I fink he fancies me!"

Flustered by my faux pas, I interjected, "No, I'm sorry, this is the wrong caravan".

I just had enough time to hear her husband reply, "bitter invoyt him in – he's too big to argue wiv," before an eruption of cheers and whooping broke out behind me. Spinning around, there in the darkness, holding torches, were about ten of the lads, all convulsed with laughter, standing besides one of the larger, more modern caravans.

I had been stitched up like a kipper by Jono, and everyone – except Jeanette and her husband – was in on it.

Jono's real caravan turned out to be quite sumptuous, but was still a squeeze for six people and I had to sleep – not much – on the floor. It seemed the hoax came about when Jono couldn't fit his car adjacent his own van, so parked alongside the 'tin of luncheon meat' – though at that time he didn't know who owned it.

After no more that three hours sleep, I felt like death warmed up the following day, especially after being woken up by Sam Kennedy banging on the side of the caravan at 5.30am. If that was a bad start, the day deteriorated when I drew next to Jono, of all people, and knew I'd have to listen to him taking the mickey out of me for five hours.

Then, en route to my peg on the Snake, I had to abandon my trolley after one of the wheels dropped off, forcing me to hump all my tackle what seemed like a country mile. A canalised water with over 100 pegs to chose from, the Snake was nevertheless well matured with plenty of trees, features and reeds along its length. It also varied in width from six metres to 12 metres depending where you were pegged.

I drew an end peg, where it was about 11 metres wide. For once it seemed the Gods were shining on me and Jono's constant jibes about sitting alongside 'Mr Blank' dried up after I had netted four plump commons to his one crucian during the first hour or so. I also hooked an absolute lump, which tanked off into the underwater reed stems on the far side. My size 16 bungee stretched further than Dawn French's knicker elastic, and then disintegrated. That set me back, as my only other power top contained a dual elastic arrangement with no's 5 and 10 threaded through it. Still, I soldiered on, and added two more small mirror carp, plus some roach, to my tally, before I caught my hook in the mesh of the keepnet.

Re-positioning your keepnet during a match is not the wisest thing to do, however I had no option but to partially gather it in to enable me to reach the snagged hook.

The bottom of the net, though, was itself caught on something on the bottom. I gave it a pull and it came free, enabling me to reach and remove the barbless hook from the mesh, before it sank back into the water. By the end of the match I had silenced Jono once and for all, and could even have been in with a chance of winning on a day when the Snake canal was not at its best.

"What have you had Peter?" enquired our irascible match secretary Ken, as I started to withdraw my net from the water. "Maybe 20lbs," I replied confidently. Imagine therefore how I felt when I pulled out a totally empty keepnet, with a sizeable rip in the bottom.

Jono was beside himself, and did a jig of delight on the bank. He then proceeded to tell anyone who would listen that I actually blanked yet again, and that my supposed '20lbs catch' was a figment of my fertile imagination.

Sickened by my bad luck, it proved a long drive home – especially after I discovered just 12lbs won the match! Chris tried to console me by telling me about the day he missed out on winning the national Land Registry championship at Tingrith in Bedfordshire after a big tench slid from his hands as he tried to place it in his keepnet. I suppose you have to endure the bad days in order to appreciate the good ones.

I did have the last laugh on Jono a year later, after I

was again unlucky enough to be pegged next to him, this time on the match lake at Border Fisheries, near Crewe. I got 22lbs to his 5lbs and watched with great amusement as his only top three was dragged into the lake by a greedy carp in the margins while he rummaged in his carryall for a reel.

Scooting across the surface it eventually tipped up, like the Titanic, before slowly disappearing beneath the surface forever.

Whistling 'God save the Queen' Jono stood to attention and saluted as he watched it go under. That was the last time we saw him.

A few years later another club member, Ben Topham, lost a top set at Border Fisheries in identical circumstances, but showed a deal more initiative by commandeering a boat and rowing out into the middle of the lake to retrieve his pole top, and the carp, before it sank.

As you might expect I have also lost a top three of my pole, but in my case, in much more mysterious circumstances. Fishing the match pool at Docklow one afternoon with Chris, it was more than unusually slow so I decided the time was right to leave the fishing, and go shopping in Leominster for provisions. Breaking down my pole and placing the top three on a pole roost alongside my box, well away from the waters edge, I made sure all my bait boxes were covered over. I didn't want any of the bird life helping themselves, as they were prone to do, when pegs were left unsupervised.

I must have been gone for around two hours and during that time Chris said only one other fellow angler had passed by, yet when I returned, my top three had vanished. I searched my peg, and the adjacent bushes, but could find no sign of it. Theft is always a possibility but that is not the sort of thing you would ever expect from residents staying at Docklow. It was a complete mystery, and even Docklow owner Mike Bozward couldn't explain it, though he did say that anglers often reported the loss of pole tops and they concluded carp had dragged them into the lake.

The loss of my top three remained a puzzle for another six months until Mike's son, Simon, who runs the tackle shop, told me in all seriousness they had found what appeared to be a peacock's nest about 100 yards from the lake. Apparently, it included pieces of broken and crushed pole tips and sections, all intertwined with bits of elastic, sticks and line.

Now, I may be a sucker for a cock and bull story but even I found this outrageous tale hard to swallow, but Simon swears blind it is true. Who am I to argue?

I rang Chris to tell him of Simon's discovery. "A peacock? A peacock! He repeated incredulously. "Well, you know what they say, there's very few nests that haven't seen a cock or two, and that story sounds like a load of them!"

Chapter 18
A brush with the Grim Reaper

Ask anyone who doesn't fish what image it conjures in the mind, and most will choose words like 'restful' and 'relaxing'. Some of course, subscribe to the theory fishing is the art of doing almost nothing and believe it must be thoroughly boring.

Few though, would ever associate the pastime with having a heart attack. But on Sunday 13th – yes, that day again – of December 1998 that's exactly what happen to me, at the comparatively young age of 47. Now of course, it wasn't the simple act of fishing, which brought about this life-threatening crisis. That was precipitated by a combination of smoking, unhealthy eating, being overweight, and a stressful lifestyle, but the actual catalyst on the day was sheer physical effort.

It must have been around 10.00am that I made a snap decision to go fishing on the club ponds, and was in the process of lugging all my gear up two fields, to a group of small ponds which sat on the crown of a hill, when I was confronted by a muddy quagmire in front of a farm gate. Trying to negotiate my way through, I found myself sinking deeper into the mire, and was struggling to extricate myself. After straining every sinew, I dragged myself out, but was, not unsurprisingly, in a lather of sweat by the time I arrived at the pond and dropped my gear down by my chosen peg.

Though the air temperature can have been no more than 6–7 degrees centigrade, I stripped off my jacket and jersey as I set up my pole. In an effort to calm myself I even lit a cigarette and chilled out for a moment. It would be my last.

Conscious my breathing was becoming laboured, I stubbed out the cigarette as the discomfort in my chest became evermore acute and was accompanied by a tingling sensation in my left arm. Before long, it felt as if someone had their boot on my chest and was trying to crush my rib cage.

By this time I knew I was in trouble, and what's more there was no one to help me beside a deserted pond, ½ mile from the road, on a chilly and dank December morning. If only I possessed a mobile phone. The phrase 'shitting one's self' may well be a crude euphemism for loss of bowel control caused by panic, but there is no other way to describe the physical symptoms of a sudden urge at a moment like that. I relieved myself in the bushes along side the pond before packing up my gear. Somehow, I had to get down to the road and summon help.

With the pain in my chest now excruciating, I staggered over the stile and stumbled down the field, panting for breath. Everything was spinning around me. After rolling over a small barbed wire fence, I struggled to my feet and staggered a few more paces before falling flat on my back, clutching my chest, in the middle of the field.

As I lapsed in and out of consciousness, I remember thinking, 'What an inglorious end, in a field full of cow pats.' Then I thought of my family, and told myself, 'No, you must keep going, if you stop here you will surely die before anyone finds you.'

Somehow, I crawled to the gate and literally collapsed onto the narrow country road, about ten yards from my parked car. I remember hearing a voice I recognised. It was one of the younger members, Andy Rankin, who apparently ran off to get help at the nearby farm. There was a girl, too, on a horse, talking on a mobile phone. Then there were paramedics and other people. My chest felt as though it was about to explode.

Talk about 'wake up with a crowd around you'. The rest is a blur, although I do recall snapping at the paramedic in the back of the ambulance for trying to cut open my expensive fishing suit with a pair of scissors. Apparently, I was covered in cow dung.

By the time the two-tone horns stopped, Maria was waiting for me at the Accident and Emergency entrance to our local hospital when I emerged from the ambulance, wearing an oxygen mask, and connected to some sort of monitor. According to the doctors, I had cheated the Grim Reaper by minutes.

After showing her the thumbs up to prove I was still alive, my first words were evidently to the effect of "ask Jonesy to go and get my gear from the pond".

After three days in the hands of the intensive care angels in the cardiac care unit, I went out onto the ward to begin my long period of rehabilitation, which would commence with a cold, and analytical, examination of my life style.

At the time, my average working week was around 70 hours, comprising some 36 as manager of the Technical section of Mersey Tunnels, and the balance producing and editing match programmes for Rovers.

To compound matters, my second book on the history of Tranmere Rovers had just been published, and my life was a whirlwind of book signings and radio interviews promoting Christmas sales.

I was also working to tight deadlines to deliver all the copy for three 40 page programmes over the holiday period before the printers closed down for the break. Add that level of stress to an unhealthy diet, being substantially overweight, and smoking, and I was classic heart attack material – or myocardial infarction as it is more correctly called.

After discussing the future with Maria, I resigned immediately as programme editor, ceased all the freelance writing for newspapers and magazines, packed in smoking, and went on a health trip and diet.

My family and friends were wonderfully supportive, and at one stage I was overwhelmed with visitors and well-wishers, including messages from Tranmere supporters whom I did not know personally, but had seemingly touched their lives. It was quite a humbling experience.

On the other hand, the message from my mates at the angling club was "get off your fat arse and get out there fishing again". Meanwhile, old pal Ken Gouldson told me a he had found a buyer for my slippers if they were going to be no use to me.

But the funniest thing that happened in hospital was when I went for a walk on the ward one night, and the old boy in the next bed, having wet his own, got into mine instead, and promptly crapped all over my bedclothes and my reading specs. Sounds like the kind of thing that happens to Victor Meldrew doesn't it? 'I didn't believe it either.' Though I spent three months off work recuperating, I was back on the bank fishing, with the help of Chris, Jonesy, Jono and the lads, by the last day of January, a mere six weeks after my brush with the Grim Reaper.

While I had home visits from other members of the club, some bearing gifts of angling books to read, one of the most welcome visitors was Ian Courtney. After years of infrequent contact, because we moved in differing angling circles, ironically it took a heart attack to re-unite us. Although it took several months of rehabilitation, I was fit as a fiddle – and a lot lighter – by summer when Chris and I (plus Jonesy for a few days) embarked on our annual pilgrimage to Docklow.

Considering the time of year, the weather was truly awful, with humid conditions and daily thunderstorms. Because Mike likes the fishery to look as natural as possible, there are no man-made pegs around many of the lakes. This is fine until it rains heavily and all the ground and clay paths become a sea of mud, and you have nowhere to clean and dry out all your gear and clothing.

Once again I failed to catch a 'double', my biggest of the week scaling only 9½lbs, but I did have one fateful encounter with a fish that may well have been twice that size…

While Chris, still on a high from winning the weekly residents' match, predictably fished his favourite match pool; Jonsey, who stayed with us for a couple of nights, and I tried the Snake, at last taking advantage of a break in the weather.

After a less than enthralling few hours, Jonesy went for a walk and came back with news that the carp, which days earlier had been spawning, were feeding their heads off amid clouds of mud in the Figure of Eight pool. Jonesy moved first, and by the time I decided to join him, had already caught several to around 6lbs on baked beans. Knowing I desperately needed a good day to round off a largely disappointing week,

Mark invited me to sit fairly close to him, alongside the wooden bridge that separates the Figure of Eight from the Micky Mouse pool, because that was where the carp seemed to be shoaled up.

Because we were sitting closer together than we would normally, we agreed that should either of us hook a real lump the other would give him a clear run until the fish was landed. Within minutes I found I was into fish and was bagging up on carp between 3 and 5lbs, with one, a perfectly scaled common, just topping 8lbs.

Jonesy was set to go home around lunchtime so Chris came over to say goodbye.

Around the same time, an amiable London match angler by the name of Terry Fuller, who we had chatted to all week, stopped by, as he and his wife walked around the lakes. Tel had been telling us the previous night about his 14.5m pole, which cost £1600, and how balance was more important than weight.

"Have a go with my pole," I offered, "and tell me what you think of the balance compared to your expensive one. Is it really £1,000 worse?"

Sitting on my box, Tel extended the pole to 13 metres and added the extension, to take the rig and hook, which was bare, save a tiny sliver of baked bean left from the last fish I'd landed, right over to the reeds by the bridge.

Tel lifted the rig in and out a few times, then pretended to strike. "It's not baad at ferteen meaters, " was his verdict, "but it's a bit cumbersome and vague aufter that. I wouldn't fancy holdin' it at vis lenff for foive hours."

Tel let the rig settle by the reeds and made a helpful comment about the visibility of my float. I turned to see Jonesy slipping the net under another fat common.

"Hey up my son," said Tel, "you've 'ad a take here," and handed the pole back to me. Surely not on a bare hook I thought! The fish moved rapidly along the edge of the reeds, thankfully in the opposite direction to the bridge, the No 14 elastic cutting a fluorescent pink swathe through the chocolate coloured water.

"It feels big," I announced excitedly. Certainly, I didn't sense it was foul hooked. That jag, jag sensation and lack of control always gives the game away. For a moment I thought the fish, which was stoically hugging the bottom and throwing up a trail of mud in its wake, was going to bottom out my elastic, so I sunk a good five metres of the tip under water, said a quick prayer to the God of monofilament, closed my eyes and held on for dear life.

Much to my surprise the expected twang of broken 6lbs high tech line, or elastic, never materialised, and when I lifted the pole the fish was in front of me. Seeing my chance to gain the initiative, I quickly broke the sections down to about eight metres, and felt as if I had the fish under control as it circled endlessly in front of me.

"Your doin' foine my son," said Tel encouragingly, while Chris, standing behind me, urged "just take your time and don't try to bully him."

For 15 minutes the fish circled in front of me, but despite applying a modicum of steady pressure, I still couldn't coax it off the bottom. Nevertheless, the vortex created by it's rudder like tail told me this was undoubtedly a potential personal best, and maybe even larger than the 'King'. Certainly, the lake was known to contain some 'twenties'.

To my right, I noticed Jonesy, having pulled out as agreed when I hooked the big fish, had restarted fishing again at about three metres out, anxious to make the best use of his remaining time before he had to leave. I flashed him a warning glance that could have sliced through a side of ham. "You've got it under control now, where's the harm?" he retorted defensively.

Just then Jonesy hooked another of those small, rocket propelled carp, which hared off to his left, but was not going to get too far against the tension of his number 18 elastic. Whether it was the presence nearby of another panicking fish, or just a question of mine getting a second wind, we will never know, but my monster suddenly tore off like a demon right across the path of Jonesy's fleeing three pounder.

For a brief moment there was a clash of taut line and then all went slack, as a small dibber float entwined in a 139 turn water knot arrowed past me into the tree branches behind!

For a moment or two there was silence as we all absorbed the enormity of the loss I had sustained. "I'm sorry mate, I truly am," proffered Jonesy apologetically. Putting my pole down, I put my head in my hands, unable to speak, or comprehend what had just happened. I felt physically sick. "I virtually had it in the bag and it was massive," I whined. "I never felt I'd lose it until…" I didn't finish the sentence.

Tel and Chris tried to console me. "It's just one of those things. It could have taken fright at any time. Better to have hooked and lost, than not hooked at all."

"That's bollocks!" I retorted. Nothing they could say could make me feel any better. Jonesy, clearly mortified by what he had done, apologised again, "I'm gutted mate, I really am. It was my fault, sorry."

Deciding it was best to beat a hasty retreat, he packed up his gear and departed for home.

It took me some time to regain my composure and get over the overwhelming sense of disappointment. As far as I'm concerned, an opportunity to catch a fish like that comes along once in a lifetime for the pole angler, and to this day I still believe I would have landed it without the intervention of Jonesy's last 'put in'.

But I have long since forgiven him his indiscretion, and we remain close friends and fishing partners. I would never allow a fish, of all things, to come between us. We were reminiscing, as you do, at the club hotpot supper recently and the subject of Docklow and 'that fish' arose. While Jonesy again pleaded guilty and begged forgiveness, Chris surprised me saying, "We all thought you were going to have another heart attack when you lost that one. You looked like death warmed up."

Recalling both occasions vividly, and the differing types of pain I felt, a coincidence struck me. "Mark, what did you just say your new pole is called?"

"The Grim Reaper," he replied, sipping on his pint.

I afforded myself a little chuckle. "Remind me not to fish next to you again! I've had a brush with him before, and given your track record, I don't fancy another".

Chapter 19

It never happened to Mr Crabtree

Anglers love nothing more than to believe in the power of 'secret' baits. Find yourself pegged next to someone who appears to be fishing in the same manner, but is bagging up while you stare the dreaded 'blank' full in the face, and it is tempting to conclude he must be using a 'secret' bait or attractant.

Now, flavourings are huge business these days, with those who manufacture them claiming their use will enhance catch rates dramatically. The salient point such exponents fail to make clear is, that if there *are* no fish in your swim, nor likely to be, because it lacks the necessary fish holding features or underwater topography, no amount of secret bait, or attractant, is going to bring the fish in front of you.

Secondly, if fish *are* in front of you, and in the mood to feed, you can present the oldest, toughest and smelliest maggot in the bait tin and they'll wolf it down. Designer flavourings are not necessary, because fish are neither intelligent nor sophisticated. That said, on days when the going is tough, and lots of people are using the same bait – luncheon meat or corn for example – it can pay to enhance your offering with an alternative colour or aroma to encourage the more discerning diner to select the chaff from the wheat.

Over the years I have come up with the odd

concoction myself ranging from rancid cheese paste to sweet smelling gelatine pellets. Some have worked, but if I am honest I have often adopted a perfunctory attitude to bait preparation tending to follow others rather than be too innovative myself. This of course has led to some real duffers...

One of our senior members, Ken Mooney, once tipped me off about his favourite 'secret' bait to catch crucians – sultanas soaked in rum! According to Ken, they hooked well and the rum permeated the water to send the crucians into a drunken feeding frenzy. He must have been tipsy when he told me, or used a different brand to me, because I never had so much as one bite on them and ended up eating them myself, and drinking the remains of the bottle.

Tipping a red maggot with a quarter of a tinned button mushroom was another clever ruse passed onto me by a matchman in whispered tones. No doubt he wet himself later telling his mates that he had just persuaded a gullible pleasure angler to buy a tin of button mushrooms and use them as bait. 'Magic mushrooms' they certainly weren't. Perhaps, he owned a mushroom farm and was looking for ways to increase sales.

Some of the most bizarre things do catch fish though. Though far from easy to keep on the hook, Chris has caught carp and chub off the top using pink marshmallows, while I've had good days using macaroni and even baked beans as bait. I also know people that have caught barbel and chub from the River Severn in Shrewsbury using deep fried chips. If you think of the logic, it isn't too surprising really. Late night revellers regularly throw their chip wrappers off the bridge into the river as they stagger home.

The most unusual bait, and I use the term loosely, I

have ever seen anyone catch on was a piece of rubber eraser, soaked in trout pellet oil. This guy, at Whiteacres in Cornwall, claimed the fish couldn't tell the difference between that and luncheon meat, and that the eraser stayed on the hook longer! I'm not sure 'Mr Crabtree' would have approved. Nevertheless, it is clearly possible to catch with whatever you have in your pocket at the time.

At Hickory Hollow, I once caught a 13lbs carp on two sugary fruit pastilles on a hair rig, while a couple of chunks of white Bourneville chocolate, threaded onto a size 6 hook, fooled a nine pound common at Docklow.

It's all very well dabbling with flavours just as long as you can get the smell off your hands afterwards. I once bought a phial of Rod Hutchinson's 'Secret Agent' elixir, which has the most pungent curry smell imaginable. Despite taking precautions not to get it on my hands, I inevitably did so. The grimace on Maria's face told me it was objectionable, but despite scrubbing my hands with every hand cleanser known to man, for fully two weeks, shop staff, barmaids and work colleagues looked down their noses at me with utter disdain. Sorry, Mr Hutchinson, but I won't be using that product again! If humans find me so repulsive they won't venture within ten yards, what chance have I with fish?

In the last five years I have enjoyed considerable success – by my standards – fishing paste and pellets in the margins. If I can catch fish using this method anyone can.

I owe my relative accomplishment to Jonesy, who has perfected the technique to such an extent, he has won a few matches and earned himself the nickname, 'Mr Paste-ry'. Having initially been duped into buying someone else's 'secret' paste mixture for about £10 per kilo, only for it to turn out to be no better than scolded and mashed trout pellets, we have developed our own version that can be adapted to suit fishery rules. There are no secret ingredients though. It is bait presentation that counts, and we have proved it can work as well during the winter as it does in the summer, just as long as you reduce the size of the lump used and its food content.

More important than the actual composition, is the consistency, and rate at which the paste will dissolve. We find many shop-bought pastes are far too stiff. The object of the exercise is to create a substance that a hook will pull through easily and dissolve within a few minutes leaving a trail of smells and particle appetisers on the bottom to support the regular introduction of pellets.

When moulded around a large hook, I find paste most effective when critically balanced, meaning that it is fished at dead depth so the float is almost being dragged under by the weight – like a plummet. The bites using this technique are generally very positive, and on some days when they are really having it, they can literally drag your pole or rod or off its rest.

Such a prospect is one reason why I have never been enamoured by the 'method', where the favoured approach is to mould a thick groundbait or paste, laced with goodies, around a frame feeder and then bury the hookbait within. It may be deadly on waters where it is permissible, but it is equally pernicious to fish which can end up tethered to a heavy feeder at best and at worst a complete rod and reel. On that score, I speak from experience. At Cudmore Fishery in Staffordshire, I lost an expensive heavy feeder rod and Shimano reel in just such circumstances. Fishing Milo lake where carp grow to mid-doubles, the strong cross winds brought me into contact with the overhead power lines which dissect the lake, prompting a switch from open-end feeder to it's heavier cousin, the method feeder.

When the bites come on 'the method', they are invariably vicious, and in most cases there is no need to strike, for the weight of the feeder has already set the hook. My preferred technique was to sit on the rod butt, and wait for the tip to wrap around.

Casting 40 yards to the deeper water, I had already had two good fish when disaster struck. No sooner had the 5oz feeder hit the surface with a mighty splash, I was momentarily distracted by my companion Ben Topham, another member of our club, whose chair leg had broken plonking him on his backside.

Too busy laughing and not concentrating, I was slow to secure the butt beneath me and in that fraction of a second, the rod, still lying across my thigh, was wrenched from its rest and into the lake! Now it was Ben's turn to laugh.

There was absolutely nothing I could do as £200 worth of rod and reel skimmed over the surface before eventually sinking into the depths.

Worst of all the rod had sentimental value having been bought for me by my late father in 'exchange' for some broken blanks of my old Maver pole which he intended to recycle into the backbone of a radio controlled glider.

In terms of value, it was my biggest loss since a Great Pyrenees Mountain dog – or its owner – stood on the butt section of my pole while I was fishing the River Weaver, near Vale Royal locks six years earlier. The towpath of this particular section is unfortunately very popular with mountain bikers, dog walkers and joggers, and even joggers running with mountain dogs.

Now, mountain dogs may be delectable animals, but they also weigh as much as a Japanese sumo wrestler. As the enormous dog and its owner bounded along the towpath, there was a sickening crunch of splintered carbon as one or other of them tried to leap over the butt section of my pole, which straddled my roller, and protruded slightly over the path.

Instantly, I was up on my feet to remonstrate with the man, who was most apologetic and blamed his pet, though I suspect that had he blamed the dog unfairly for his own clumsiness, the animal would have put him right when they got home!

In fairness, the man did not quibble about the damage, and promised to pay for a replacement section, writing his address and phone number in my fishing diary.

After phoning around various tackle dealers, my lowest quote for a new butt section was £135 so I rang the dog's owner and told him. "How much?" he exploded angrily, "You've got to be fucking joking. I'm not paying that!"

"Well, that's what the end section costs, mate. A complete new pole is £650. How much did you think it would be?" I queried.

"About twenty quid, " retorted the man, adding, "and that's as much as I'm giving you.

"You can take it or leave it," he shouted, and then slammed the phone down.

Three times I tried to contact him but never got an answer, while my letter was returned 'not known at this address'. In the end, I had to claim off my household insurance. Their claims department wrote 'this sounds like a shaggy dog story'.

A work colleague of mine, Tony, had a not dissimilar

experience while fishing a match on the Leeds and Liverpool Canal near Haskayne in Lancashire. Fishing fully 14½ metres across the canal he found he could not avoid the butt section occasionally penetrating the hedge behind which separated the towpath from the adjacent houses.

When Tony went to ship the pole forward he discovered he was missing the most expensive bit of the pole.

After searching the hedge it became apparent it wasn't wedged in the foliage, so Tony resolved to complete the last hour of the match and then go around to the house and retrieve it. It wasn't easy to identify the correct property, but in the end he knocked on the door of a neat semi and politely asked if the butt section of his pole had dropped off into the garden.

"No, it didn't drop off, I pulled it off," retorted the man angrily. "How would you like that fucking thing coming through the hedge and poking you in the ear while you are trying to have a kip in the garden?"

"OK, I'm sorry," said Tony politely. "You've made your point, now can I have the end of my pole back please?

"No you bleedin' can't," growled the house owner, intransigently. "It's on my property and that's where it's staying." He slammed the front door, leaving Tony to contemplate his next move.

Noticing the car in the drive of his house had the sunroof wide open, Tony went to his car and took out a bait box containing around two pints of pinkies. He then returned to the house and rang the doorbell again. Mr Grumpy appeared.

"I'll give you a choice mate," said Tony, holding the box over the open sunroof, "either I get my pole section back, or all these maggots are going in your car." Faced with the prospect of tit for tat retaliation, Mr Grumpy suddenly had a change of heart and within a few minutes Tony had the butt end of his pole back!

Given these sort of skirmishes, there is a lot to be said for fishing your own private club waters, or even commercial fisheries, where you don't encounter fluctuating water levels, tackle jackals, mad cows, angry swans, bulls, giant dogs, joggers, cyclists and grumpy neighbours. In that respect, our club waters are the perfect retreat, and are probably better stocked than some commercial and syndicate fisheries. Aside from the usual species, we also have some interesting 'illegal immigrants' in the shape of goldfish, a brown trout and even a terrapin, which someone dumped over the fence.

A cluster of beautiful 100-year-old plus ponds surrounded by mature trees and bushes, they are dotted around lush fields, and are rented from the tenant dairy farmers.

The biggest water is just over half an acre in size. Through the hard work of committee, and membership, they are immaculately kept with purpose made pegs, fences and stiles. As they are only four miles from my home, it is easy to nip down for the last few hours of daylight during the summer evenings, which is often the most productive time to fish.

During June and early July, the club run a series of evening matches on a Tuesday, fishing 6.30pm to 10.00pm when the nights are light. With around 30 anglers scattered around the seven ponds, it's often 10.30pm before the weigh-in is completed and everyone drifts back to the club hut. In the adjacent lane, members park on a broad grass verge.

While most will fish until the 'all out', some who

have not caught – or not caught enough to win – will depart early leaving spaces in the line of parked cars by the hut. Having thoroughly enjoyed myself one evening amassing a 12lbs mixed net of modest carp, tench, crucians, skimmers, chub and roach, it was almost dark by the time I returned to the car park and was intrigued to see people encircling one particular car, looking in.

Now, normally in our part of the world, the only time you see a crowd standing around a car is when someone has spotted the owner has a valid tax disc.

Chris McGuinness beckoned me to join him, and about a dozen others, huddled around a blue Ford Escort, which had slotted in between my car and his. "Come and have a look at this," urged Chris, laughing.

Inside the car were a long-haired bloke of about 30, with several tattoos, and a beefy blond girl in her early twenties. Both were writhing around in the back completely naked, seemingly oblivious to the presence of an enthusiastic audience of voyeuristic anglers watching them perform through steamed up windows.

In fact, short of being embarrassed, they were clearly exhibitionists who relished the thrill of being watched. When the girl finally reached a shrieking climax, leaving the bloke slumped exhausted between his girlfriend's thunderous thighs, a huge cheer went up, followed by an appreciative round of applause!

Unfazed by our presence, the couple proceeded to get dressed before reversing off the grass verge and driving away, obviously delighted by their performance as 'porn stars'.

This sort of thing never happened to 'Mr Crabtree' I thought!

Chapter 20
Red letter days

Unless your name is Alan Scotthorne, and you are a world champion match angler while your wife, Sandra, holds the same title for the Ladies, the chances are you might just encounter the odd domestic difficulty with your other half regarding the real love of your life.

As anglers, we tread a fine line with our wives, girlfriends and partners. They may tolerate disappearing acts ranging from one day to a whole week, being disturbed in the small hours as we set off fishing, and even boiling hemp in the pressure cooker, but they will sure as hell draw the line at bait on the loose in the house.

A terse, shrill call from 'she who must be obeyed' was the first sign of trouble ahead as I got up that morning. "Peeeter! I think you better come downstairs". Following the voice I made my way to our utility room. A small, windowless area between the kitchen and internal door to the garage, containing a freezer, washing machine and dishwasher, plus a couple of wall mounted cupboards, I could only think there had been a flood, or the freezer had defrosted.

Instead, I followed her eyes upwards and the finger pointing at the ceiling. "Are those yours? I think you might have had an escape." My heart sank. The ceiling was covered with hundreds of tiny white maggots, about the size of squatts, defying gravity as they crawled slowly around the ceiling, while others whose balance had deserted them, had dropped onto the floor and appliances.

Through gritted teeth she made herself succinctly clear. "Get *them* out of here now!" I was baffled. I didn't have any white maggots in my small bait fridge in the garage, only red, and the container was still sealed.

In such situations I have always found blaming the dog a useful 'get out jail free' card. "Some of Tessa's dinner must have fallen down the back of the washing machine," I proffered. "If there's meat lying there and the flies have got at it…" Maria cut me short before I could explain the life cycle of the blue bottle. "I don't want to know, just get rid of them."

With the aid of a step ladder and an empty bait tin I spent the next hour plucking the little buggers off the ceiling and hunting them on the floor in all those mucky crevices that exist behind fixed domestic appliances. By 8.30am I was convinced I had rounded them all up, but could still not discover the source of the outbreak. There was nothing on the floor, or in the cupboards. Additionally, the basket of shoe polishes and the sealed polythene bag of hemp seed, on top of the cupboard seemed quite harmless. Confident that the crisis was over for the time being, I left for work.

Returning that evening Maria informed me that the infestation had returned, and yet again I did a full sweep to remove the interlopers, including those that had got under the door into the kitchen, but still couldn't find the source. That evening I virtually cleared the utility room, but still couldn't find any meat that would have given rise to the tiny maggots. Having managed to block off a high-level escape route into the kitchen, I transferred every box, container and bag into the garage for examination and there, to my surprise, eventually discovered the source.

Inside the bag of old hemp seed there were hundreds of maggots. Seemingly, they escaped through a small puncture onto the top of the wall cupboard and then onto the ceiling.

Quite how they propagated inside that plastic bag we will never know, but even when they were removed, domestic bliss was not quite restored, for in two weeks time those that had escaped my clutches turned to tiny flies, and once again, I was in trouble over fishing.

After spending a fortune at Docklow on baits such as maggots and worms that like to wriggle free, according to Jonesy, the only thing I would need for our projected trip to Whiteacres in Cornwall, was a 25kg bag of trout pellets, plus a few tins of corn and cat food.

Having just about reached the end of my tether with the bird life at Docklow, and become increasingly frustrated by my inability to catch from the match pool, I was more than ready for a change of holiday venue, and hopefully, luck. Thus four of us, Jonesy, Ben Topham, Chris and myself booked one of the luxury caravans at Whiteacres Holiday Park near Newquay, a site designed specifically for anglers and their families.

Though it was to be a new experience for Chris and I, both Ben and Jonesy had been there before with their families and knew 'the score', as they say. But when it came to the crunch of paying, Chris dropped out, leaving my old pal, and carp fanatic, Garry Doolan to take his place. While some of Whiteacres' pools had too much of that recently 'dug out' look – with saplings wearing dog collars – I found Bolingey lake near Perranporth much more to my liking.

Exclusive to Whiteacres residents only, we spent more time there, and at the prolific nearby day ticket fishery called Gwinear, than we did on the waters adjacent to the caravan park.

Nestling in a picturesque valley, Bolingey is a beautiful, secluded and reed fringed lake, with two arms and islands, generously framed by mature trees and foliage. It is stocked largely with mirrors, commons and ghosties up to 27lbs, plus quality roach.

On my first visit, I enjoyed a real red-letter day with over 120lbs of carp to 9lbs, using paste and pellet tactics close in, to earn a new nickname, courtesy of Jonesy, of the 'Butcher of Bolingey'.

Indeed, in each of my subsequent visits during the week I also caught over 100lbs, but strangely, no single fish exceeding 9lbs. Even though it was virtually all carp, you never knew what species it would be, nor size, and the sport could be phenomenal right through the day until 7.00pm when the gates closed.

One of the most remarkable sights I have ever seen in 40 years angling was a common carp approaching 20lbs, head completely out of the water, sucking pellets out of the overhanging grass just minutes after I had packed up, seemingly oblivious to my crouching presence a few feet away.

Now given Jonesy had netted fish to 14½lbs, Ben to 11½lbs, and Garry a splendid 19½lbs specimen using out and out carp tactics, the fact that I still could not catch a double, as opposed to watching one, had not, should we say, gone without comment from the others. Even Jonesy's pony-tailed mate, John Stepton, a match angler from Romford, who was known simply as 'Cockney John', joined in the mickey taking at every opportunity!

But he decided to 'laive it owt' after I got my own back pointing out the camera with which he had just asked me to photograph his new personal best carp of 14lbs, had no film in it, just seconds after he had jubilantly returned the fish to the water.

The not-so-crafty cockney blamed everyone but himself, including his 'old lady', for not loading the camera, and me for not telling him until he'd put the big ghostie back.

Though thoroughly delighted with my week's tally of 90 carp to 9lbs, plus a superb 4¾lb tench, on the final day the others decided to mark my failure to break the 10lbs barrier with a special prize. In front of everyone in Whiteacres bar, I was presented with a large inflatable fish, complete with birthday sticker proclaiming, 'I am 10'. Now, I am happy to accept that as the only person not to catch a carp over ten pounds all week from venues stuffed with them, I am fair game to be ridiculed by my companions. But what hurt most was that the lads bought the inflatable on the Monday in anticipation of my failure during the week.

Like the goalscorer who couldn't find the net to save his life one season but then plunders a hat-trick on the first day of the new campaign, my return to Cornwall in June 2002 produced a few more red-letter days. After all the disappointments of Docklow, the 'butcher' had finally cracked it. With my very first put in at Bolingey I found myself engaged in titanic battle with a 'lump' of a mirror carp which stretched my No 16 elastic, 5½lbs line and 6 metre margin pole to the brink, before tipping the scales at 11lbs 4ozs. Once again, the fish fell to trout pellet paste.

And when we went to the prolific Gwinear Pools my first two fish, both taken only two feet from the platform at peg 41, weighed in at 10lbs 4ozs and 10lbs 8ozs and contributed to a catch well over the magical ton. Bizarre isn't it?

With Chris returning to the fold at the expense of Garry, our group was once again supplemented most days by the ever-competitive Cockney John, who was staying on the same site with his old lady, Tracy, and their kids. While he and Jonesy went head to head on one side of the match pool at Gwinear, weighing every fish in a deadly serious match (which 'Mr Paste-ry' won with over 200lbs!) Chris and I chose the opposite side of the lake where we could compete with the fish, rather than John.

As I did my best to put the brakes on several 'animals' as they tore off into the deep water beneath the bridge alongside peg 28, I noticed the chap opposite seemed to be having a spot of bother of his own. While I fish with tackle strong enough to give me a chance to land the fish I seek, it both amuses, and to an extent annoys me, when I see matchmen, pre-programmed to use light lines, elastic and small hooks, whatever the venue and stamp of fish it contains. After 40 minutes spent holding about 11 metres of his 14½ metre match pole up in the air, unable, because of the stretchy elastic he was using, to exert any control over the fish, this chap was achieving little except spooking everything in the adjacent swims occupied by Chris and myself.

Trying to be helpful, I suggested plunging the pole tip under the water and shipping it back slowly, as that seemed to wear them out quicker. "When I want your fucking advice I'll ask for it," was the charming reply.

Despite playing to a gallery of anglers who had already packed up, he still hadn't seen the fish after one-and-a-quarter hours, which is about the same amount of time as it takes my good lady to do the weekly shop at Tesco. In fact she could probably change a wheel on a dump truck – or even a light bulb – quicker.

Even Jonesy and Cockney John, on the opposite side of the lake, were aware of the unfolding drama, evident from calls like "has he got the bloody thing in yet? It will be dark soon…"

With his strength and patience virtually exhausted, Mr Charming finally dipped his pole beneath the surface, shipping it backwards – somewhat quicker than I would have done – and broke down at the fourth and fifth sections. Holding the former high in the air, he attempted to bully the fish to the surface.

Unfortunately, the big carp took exception and bolted, whereupon the fourth section of his lightweight match pole disintegrated with a deafening crack like a gunshot. As the crowd groaned, he simply lit up another cigarette, sighed deeply and stared wistfully at the water in front of him.

"That's your bleedin' fault!" he snarled, with a glance in my direction. That's a fresh slant on my legendary angling luck I thought. Now, I'm apparently losing fish for *other* anglers.

Despite his obnoxious attitude, I sympathised with Mr Charming on his loss. I've been there several times. As we all packed up for the night, by chance, Jonesy spoke to the same bloke in the car park without realising it was he who had lost the big fish. "How did you get on mate?" asked Mark in his usual cheery manner. The guy shook his head and replied sombrely, "I *lost* a nineteen-and-a-half-pounder. It snapped my pole after I'd played it for over an hour."

Now, *that's* what I call a proper 'fisherman's tale. Maybe he knew his pole would snap under precisely 19½lbs of pressure?

My red-letter days in Cornwall were in truth far more memorable than the day my wife and daughter Kate arranged for me as part of my 50th birthday celebrations – which included a birthday cake featuring an icing sugar angler falling in – during September 2001.

That, of course, is not a criticism of their generosity, or ingenuity, in seeking what they believed would be a very special occasion for a life-long fisherman. For the not inconsiderable sum of £150, Maria and Kate arranged for me to fish a 'carefully selected' venue containing huge carp, with coarse angling legend Bob James, who shot to prominence alongside the idiosyncratic Chris Yates in that wonderfully evocative TV series *A Passion for Angling*.

Scheduled to take place in early October at a venue called Croxley Hall in Rickmansworth, Hertfordshire, it became clear that the day would be shared with other anglers, which on the face of it I had no problem with. I wasn't expecting exclusive coaching from the maestro himself, however, by the same token, I wouldn't have booked it myself knowing I would be one of a party of over 20. Primary school classes are smaller.

Having travelled down the day before and stayed overnight in a B&B in the town, I was invited to arrive at a fishing lodge with all my gear at around 10.00am to enjoy some bacon butties and an illuminating pep talk from Bob. This proved about the most worthwhile aspect of the day.

The highest compliment I could pay Bob James is that he thinks like a fish. During his half-hour talk he certainly gave us all some food for thought on presentation and locating fish, rather than rushing to grab that favourite swim.

But after a brief demonstration, with Bob using, and promoting, his own branded rod and centre pin, under the watchful eye of his sponsors, Masterline, we were left to our own devices for the rest of the day to fish on what was clearly a very hard, weed choked lake, or alternatively, a brook full of tiddler roach. There was no coaching as such.

It didn't help that the heavens opened, and I discovered my fishing suit had lost all its waterproofing causing me to get soaked through to my underwear. But at least I didn't blank like some, catching two small roach and perch before heading back to the lodge to engage Bob in some dialogue about the filming of *A Passion for Angling*. Bob admitted the venue, and numbers were less than ideal (the venue has subsequently been changed) confirming my impression that apart from meeting the man – and having my photo taken giving him the 'benefit' of my advice – the event was a bit of a damp squib, and not just because of the weather.

In fairness to the organisers, it is probably much easier to deliver a gift experience driving a racing car or flying in a balloon. Fishing, as I can testify over the years, is far more of an unpredictable affair. In terms of fishing, I am afraid I have had better red-letter days on the Shropshire Union Canal.

Nevertheless, I did get that photograph, plus an autographed certificate, to prove I'd met Bob. I wonder if Bob got one to show he'd met me?!

Chapter 21

Winter highs and dangerous skies

Those anglers who pack away their fishing tackle as soon as autumnal winds strip bare the trees miss out on one of the most enjoyable parts of the season. Wrap up well and with just a little effort and fortitude, a few hours spent by the waterside during winter can often be more rewarding than a whole day during the summer.

Ever since I stood in the snow along the banks of the swollen River Dee in Chester as a kid, I have relished the challenge of winter fishing on small rivers and still waters – providing they aren't frozen. In this respect, the River Dane, which flows through Cheshire before discharging into the River Weaver in Northwich town centre can be a real joy in winter, but like all small rivers you must do your homework before travelling, as a few days rain can raise levels dramatically.

Indeed, I recall fishing the Croxton Lane section, near Middlewich, one November, and having to contend with a large wicker settee, complete with cushions, that some cretin had obviously dumped in the river. Carried into my swim by the swirling floodwater, it lodged against a partially submerged tree branch right in front of me as I tried to cajole a chub or two from the same spot. Now I know what is meant by the phrase 'armchair swim'. I gave up and moved.

One of the reasons for my enthusiasm for small rivers was the urge to complete, so to speak, the full set of indigenous coarse fish with the 'lady of the stream' – the beautiful grayling. For years the species eluded me, and despite fishing the upper reaches of the Severn, Dee, and Dane, it was not until last year that I joyously slid my net under the first of three pristine grayling around 1¼lbs apiece.

They were taken whilst wading on a private stretch of the picturesque River Vyrnwy near Llanymynech in north Wales. As I stared down at the pristine fish lying in my net, a whoop of delight cut through the first chill of autumn, and scattered a family of wood pigeons nesting in the pine trees opposite.

For a moment I was tempted to take the fish back to the bank to record its capture on celluloid for posterity – fundamentally to prove to Jonesy I had finally laid to rest a long time hoodoo. But fearing the delicate fish might not survive the trauma, I returned it, with a kiss, to the rushing water immediately. It was not the time for self-indulgence, and I don't use keep nets these days unless fishing a match. Why deprive a fish of its liberty in the name of vanity?

The previous winter, Jonesy and I had fished the tiny River Alyn at Rossett near Wrexham a few days post Christmas when the banks were blanketed in snow, after we heard on the grapevine grayling to over 2lbs were being taken on trotted maggot.

But the day we arrived, the river was really tanking through and despite checking my centre pin to hold back my chubber float so the maggots would flutter enticingly in the fast current, I could not induce any of the residents, let alone grayling, to bite.

After twice getting tangled up in the overhanging

trees, and losing another rig on an annoying snag downstream, I resorted to a one-ounce lead cast under-arm to hold a bunch of maggots. But it did me no good, I still blanked.

Picture how I felt therefore, when Jonesy, fishing about 30 yards downstream of me, caught a magnificent gray-ling of well over 2lbs just seconds after poking the tip of his pole into a slack and holding his rig relatively still in the flow. I love my pole, but only a Philistine would use one on a river like the Alyn.

Though there was snow on the ground that day, the temperatures were tolerable for a few hours at least, and that, empirically, is probably the key to winter fish-ing. Even when it has frozen overnight the better stamp fish seem to feed, albeit briefly, when the sun warms the water by maybe a degree or so, often around lunch-time. Thus, I have often found a short session between 11.30am and 3.00pm to be the most productive, particu-larly on still waters.

While a good proportion of my winter fishing is spent on my own club waters, when they were out of bounds during the Foot and Mouth outbreak of 2001, together with most running water in the region, I switched my attention to Cheshire Fishing. The Tattenhall complex – one of the few not on farmland – remained open throughout the crisis.

If ever there was a place to test the quality of your fishing gear this is it. With no proper paths or pegs, a week of sustained rain can turn the banks into a quag-mire, while the upper lakes, including the trout pools, are especially exposed to the cold easterly winds.

Apart from lightning, of all the other elements, I find wind is the angler's biggest enemy – and I don't mean the type that clears a room. Unless you are a masochist with unlimited wealth, fishing the long pole in strong cross winds is an act of madness. Umbrellas, too, tend to perish in such conditions and during those months at Cheshire I lost two of them.

The first blew inside out, breaking all the spines and tipping over my box, to which it was connected, plus bait, as I tried desperately to nail down the guy ropes. After shelling out another 50 quid, the second brolly, supposedly designed to hug the ground and be pegged down, was also consigned to the dustbin when the centre pole twisted and distorted after an exceptionally violent gust.

If I might digress, it has to be said the quality and durability of many accessories manufactured for anglers today is questionable to say the least. I have lost count of the number of rod holdalls and carryalls I have had which have either rotted or the supposedly indestructible zip has self-destructed. By contrast, the canvas and leather rod holdall I bought when I was 20 was still going strong when I gave it away ten years ago.

While Cheshire Fishing may not be the best place to be during a sudden snowstorm, that is often mitigated by the quality of the winter fare. A well-established and truly mixed fishery, pool one, a rectangular water maybe 30 metres wide, is reputed to contain several roach between 2 and 2½lbs.

Given my lifelong quest to break the two-pound barrier for that species, my winter campaign centred on achieving that target. After much experimentation with maggot, caster, pinkies and even squatt, I reached the conclusion that feeding small balls of worm flavoured black groundbait laced with chopped worm, via a pole pot, offered the best chance of attracting large roach to my swim. I also found I got more positive bites if

I scaled down, presenting a piece of worm on a size 22 hook to 1½lbs hook link, in conjunction with a dual elastic system of No 5 to 10 through my top three.

During the first couple of sessions I could not catch roach any bigger that 12 ounces, and was plagued by small skimmers. However, a subtle change to the shotting pattern reaped rich rewards. In one manic 15 minute spell, I caught roach of 1lbs 2oz, 1lbs 4oz, two of 1lbs 6ozs, one of 1½lbs, and a new personal best of 1lbs 10ozs, in successive put ins.

Sadly, no fish over 2lbs graced my net, but as a catch it remains one of the highlights of my angling life. Proof, at last, that I can catch quality fish occasionally. But that was not the only excitement that chilly February day. Almost inevitably as the temperature rose a couple of degrees during the afternoon when the cloud broke to reveal a low winter sun, so the carp found my chopped worm feed and bullied the roach into moving on. Half suspecting that might happen, I had just upped my hooklength strength to 2lbs and increased the hook size to a 20, when the dotted down red tip of my float buried and I found myself connected to something definitely not a roach.

Obstinately holding bottom, the big fish tugged and stretched my elastic to the point of bottoming out, necessitating the use of all 14 metres of pole. Initially, it went left, and then turned tail heading off to my right, and all I could do was follow it down the lake. This pantomime went on for fully 30 minutes before the chap fishing opposite, with rod and line, grabbed his rod as it appeared to be yanked off its rest by a big fish. "Nearly lost that," he shouted. Within seconds it became noticeable that whichever direction my taut elastic stretched, so the other chap's float and line followed. Bizarrely, it seemed we were both connected to the same fish.

"You must have foul hooked it," I called out. "I'll cut my line," he offered generously, and promptly did so allowing me to once again take control. Gradually, I broke down the pole until the fish was circling in front of me, but could not chance exerting any pressure to get its head up in case the hooklength snapped.

After fully 45 minutes I finally slid the net under a long, sleek common carp, which tipped the scales at 10½lbs, and to my amazement found it hooked in a barbule, rather than lip. The angler opposite had somehow managed to hook my fish in the tail. "I couldn't have done that if I'd tried," he observed, as I handed back his float and terminal tackle.

A few weeks later the fishery provided another test of my mettle. Once again intent on fishing for roach, I arrived to find most of the pools frozen over after a particularly hard night's frost.

The ice on pool two, the largest on the complex, seemed the thinnest, and therefore most likely to break, so with the help of another angler armed with a heavy weight and rope, I carved myself a swim about three metres wide by eight metres. Despite introducing a regular drip feed of casters, after two hours all I had to show for my efforts were two skimmers, a small and pale crucian that was obviously seasonally confused, and a pair of blue hands.

The thought of carp feeding during such cold conditions never crossed my mind, but when my tiny float buried with indecent haste, and the No 6 elastic streaked out of my pole tip, I was forced to revise my appraisal of the day's fishing potential.

All I could do was hang on, and plunge the pole under

water, shipping as much as I could beneath the ice and angle it to the left, and then right, depending on which side the fish seemed – and its very difficult to tell – to be pulling from. My difficulties were exacerbated by renegade chunks of floating ice, which seemed to attach themselves to my elastic as it retracted.

Eventually, the fish was cajoled from under the ice into my swim and after an eternity paddling around in ever decreasing circles, finally came to the net. An ounce under seven pounds, I still regard its capture as an achievement in the circumstances. Last season, one of our club members, Nick Price, fishing in identical conditions, landed a fish twice that size to win a Winter League match – a testimony to his angling skill.

Our club waters often turn up surprises during the winter. Fishing opposite another member, Bill Sharp, on a pit near the lane, we were both conscious of something swimming around the pond just under the surface.

Too big to be a water rat, and too fleet to be a relation of the rogue terrapin which someone dumped in one of our other ponds, it was a bit of a puzzle. There was a commotion in the water next to Bill's keepnet. "It's attacking my fucking net," exclaimed Bill adding, "I'm sure it's an otter."

I ran around the pond in time to see the long bushy tail of a mink break the surface. Despite laying traps, no one has ever seen it again, so it was presumably passing through the farm fields that are home to both our waters, and the local model aircraft club, that included my late father among its members.

Since my heart attack, during wintertime I now tend to stick to the ponds nearest the road, where I often ran into my father wandering the fields, flying his radio controlled planes and gliders.

One day his genial face appeared over the hedge alongside the pond where I was fishing. "Hi, I don't suppose you could give me a bit of help? The car is stuck in the mud in the flying field." I put down my rod and accompanied him through the gate and over the stile and there, buried up to the wheel hub in mud, was his silver Volkswagen Polo, surrounded by his planes and paraphernalia.

After much fruitless pushing, rocking and shoving, my father produced a towrope from his boot and suggested I reverse my own, more powerful, car into the field and pull him out.

This I did without too many problems, but as soon as I hitched up the Polo and started to accelerate, the wheel spin rapidly dug a trough in the soft ground for my car to sink into, which left us both stuck! We eventually owed our freedom to the tenant farmer, and her labourers, who appeared with a tractor and after a tug of war, pulled us both out. Is that what they mean by 'field sports' I wondered?

Before his sudden death in late December 2002, my father spent many hours flying his various radio controlled model planes in that field. He often told me of the damage they sustained when the engine stalled, or were caught in thermals and carried out of range of the controller, eventually falling to ground. Apparently, the engine and rudder mechanism were the only recoverables when they crashed.

One unseasonably warm Sunday afternoon in February I was sitting besides the same pond I had been fishing when I had my heart attack up on the crest of the hill, listening with no small measure of irritation, to the incessant whine of the model aircraft engines as they zoomed around the skies above me. "It's like being on the film set of 633 Squadron," said the chap opposite, adding, "I wish I had a ground-to-air missile!" Much as I tried to ignore the dogfights and loops, and concentrate on my float and feeding pattern, I couldn't wait for the restoration of peace and quiet when they landed for re-fuelling and 'engine tweaking'.

As tranquillity suddenly descended at last, for reasons I cannot now explain, I looked skywards just in time to see a silent plane, clearly spiralling out of control, hurtling towards the pond, and me.

It was all I could do to shout "watch out" to my companion before a large model RAF Spitfire, with a wingspan of maybe ten feet, crashed into the water vertically, right in front of me, precipitating a mini-tidal wave around the pond and sending every self-respecting fish scurrying to the far corners. By some miracle, it had missed my companion and I and our poles. With its grey balsa wood fuselage and wings broken, it lay on the surface for a moment, its engine hissing and steaming, before slowly sinking out of sight into eight foot of water. "Jesus Christ!" I exclaimed. "That could have killed us."

As we tried to collect our thoughts, my father, dressed as usual in his Barbour jacket, wellies and beret, and his friend Ray, appeared on the horizon. Approaching the far edge of the pond my father shouted, "Did you see a plane come down Peter? I think it must be up here somewhere."

At that precise moment I could have cheerfully strangled him. Now, I would give anything in the world to hear his voice again.

Chapter 22
Some things never change

When asked why he hadn't joined his local golf club, legendary American comedian Groucho Marx is reputed to have replied "I'd never wannabe a member of any club that would accept *me* as a member!" After this book, perhaps my angling club will be reconsidering whether they want me as a member.

Small in comparison with many clubs, and consequently relatively exclusive, our 55 strong membership embraces a broad spectrum of the social divides. Unlike golf clubs, your standing in the community matters not a jot. More importantly, you have to be passionate about your fishing, and willing to contribute to the wellbeing of Wirral Angling Association, as it should actually be addressed. Thus, given this diversity of membership, you can find a JCB driver fishing alongside, and chatting to, a barrister or university professor.

With such an eclectic mix of backgrounds, personalities and angling philosophies, there are bound to be a few that are prone to the odd exaggeration. You know the type. They never have a bad day, except on the occasion you sit next to them, or reckon they caught a big 'double' but never got it weighed, corroborated or photographed. Indeed, the limit of how far they can stretch truth often depends on the length of their arms! A few years ago we had a member ubiquitously nicknamed 'Larry the tench', who brazenly claimed he held the 'Welsh crucian record' with a fish of near seven pounds.

Among the fathers and sons, brothers, and brother-in-laws, and individual members, there are a few natural comedians, and a fervent sense of camaraderie, never more evident than during social get-togethers, club matches and the obligatory work parties. Given I am allocated light duties on account of my previous heart problems, I am able to admire the adeptness with which some members (Chris is an expert) avoid hard graft, and always seem to be 'nipping back to the hut for a hammer', or have a flask in their hand. A couple have even earned nicknames such as the 'wicket keeper' – he always wears big gloves but stands well back from the action – or 'blisters' because of their appearance after the hard work is over!

The real fun though starts when the boat comes out and someone tries to retrieve that long lost float entwined in an overhanging branch using a pair of long handled secateurs, only to capsize, and end up in the pond. Golfers miss out on this horseplay because caring for their own course would be considered beneath them. I somehow doubt they could have had more fun than we did when we spent the weekend in Bewdley, on the banks of the Severn, before our club match at Furnace Mill Fishery…

Nestled in a beautiful wooded glade in the Wyre Forest, Furnace Mill is owned and managed by Ed Brown, whose best pal happens to be none other than TV angling personality Matt Hayes. On the basis a spot of practice could serve as an excuse for a night out in Bewdley that evening, a posse of club members, including Chris, Jonesy, and Ben, headed down to the Midlands to fish Furnace pool.

Possibly due to the high temperatures, the big carp showed absolutely no desire to feed, and out of a dozen of us, only a couple caught. I wish I had a pound for every time someone said, "you should have been here last week mate, we were bagging up." After re-considering our tactics over a pint, we booked into our overnight accommodation, arranged by fellow member Mark Kendall, through a tackle shop in Bewdley.

Situated over a café, overlooking the River Severn and town bridge, it was at best basic, at worst, in dire need of modernisation. The bath was filthy while the carpets had more life in them than a tramps vest. Ben was furious. "Rigsby's cat wouldn't stay in this place," he moaned. With little choice, we left our gear, and headed off on a pub crawl, hoping to perhaps find angling guru Des Taylor's watering hole for a chinwag.

Arriving back at our digs, pleasantly inebriated, around midnight, having spent the last hour before dusk watching an angler catching big barbel from the embankment outside a riverside pub, I tried to draw the curtains in the room I was sharing with Chris. Not only did they fall down, so did the track and pelmet! The place was a shambles. Our attempt to get some sleep faltered though as a violent row between a man and woman erupted on the bridge outside. From the open window of the room above ours, we heard Ben's voice roar, "Shut up! Jonesy is trying to knock one out here and needs some quiet!" Chris and I mischievously encouraged them to resolve their differences in a more physical manner. "Just give her one," shouted Chris.

Of course, it wasn't long before Mr Angry was looking up at the windows above, trying to work out who was poking their nose into his argument. If he was less than enthralled by our interference, he was downright seething when Ben poured a full three-pint bait box full of cold water over his head from three floors up. At least his lady-friend was pleased though. She teetered off on her high heels shrieking with laughter. "Serves you right," she yelled.

To our amazement, Mr Angry was still standing outside in pugnacious mood when we came down for breakfast in the morning, but when he saw how many there were of us, he obviously thought better of a confrontation and wandered off.

As for the match, it was a real let down, won with only 15lbs by club secretary Mark Lewis. After trying just about every method I know, I managed one small roach. Some, including chairman Eddie Johnson, blanked. However, a few months later several of us, including Mark Lewis, and Eddie, returned to Furnace Mill – but not the seedy B&B – for another try, and this time the fishing was much improved. Certainly, I was pleased with carp to 8½lbs, some splendid roach, and a 5½lbs bream, while work colleague Keith Jones was delighted with a 9lbs carp off the top.

The highlight of the trip though was the sight of Eddie showing Matt Hayes's son Dan how to catch carp off the top on Mucky Meadow pool, while his dad sat chatting to Ed in the café. What's more, Eddie's 'coaching' worked and Dan immediately started hooking the cagey carp that had frustrated him.

If anyone should have been 'coaching', I suppose it should have been me, but I would never have the audacity to offer help to someone whose father is a far better angler than I could ever be. Ironically, I was probably the only qualified angling coach on the fishery that day. Only a few years ago the idea of me teaching someone else how to fish would have been laughable – some might say it still is. Indeed, it took all Jonesy's persuasive powers, and those of his friend Eddie Cardis, the

National Federation of Anglers' regional coach and organiser, to convince me I could make a fist of it.

Having told Eddie I was once compared to Bob Nudd (someone said "compared to Bob Nudd you might as well play golf."). I reluctantly agreed I would at least be able teach the rudimentary skills (except accurate casting) to beginners.

Thus persuaded, I formally applied to the NFA, and was interviewed by Frank Lythgoe at the headquarters of Warrington Anglers in the Cheshire town. Rather than recruit well-known match anglers who might not have the time or be able to handle the academic aspects of modern coaching, the NFA seem to prefer ordinary anglers who are good communicators, capable of teaching and planning formal sessions.

Though potential coaches are rightly police checked, Frank Lythgoe still likes to 'front' candidates by asking point blank "Are you a paedophile?" Though one should never be frivolous about such matters, I did wonder if there was any point, as such people go to great lengths to conceal their true colours.

After being accepted, I then underwent a formal teaching course leading to a City and Guilds certificate in 'individual learning through coaching'. The group I qualified through, including club colleague Andy Rankin, also had to put our practical teaching skills to the test with some 28 Chester school kids at Hampton Springs fishery in Cheshire in February 2001.

Given my track record, no one should be surprised that the quartet I 'coached' all blanked! In mitigation, I should point out only four of the 28 caught on a bitterly cold day and some had less than adequate tackle.

The problem the NFA have is that they have a shortage of coaches and often have no control over the numbers of children who turn up at specific sessions. With a less than desirable pupil-teacher ratio, there was a consensus of opinion it was a prosecution, or compensation claim, waiting to happen.

Shortly after I qualified, the NFA eventually decided they needed to completely revamp the way they trained coaches in order to satisfy the requirements of Sport England, the purse holders.

I decided not to bother re-qualifying, after being told I was expected to go away on 'study weekends' at my expense, prepare risk assessments for every coaching session, and fork out around £45 for an annual licence to 'permit me' to coach free of charge.

I still however help the youngsters in our club, and have taken several lapsed anglers under my wing, including Keith at work, and encouraged them to return to the bank, so feel I'm doing my bit for the future of the sport. Invariably, to help rekindle enthusiasm, I take my lapsed anglers'to commercial fisheries, simply because they offer consistent sport in an area which, excluding my club ponds, is otherwise a bit of a coarse fishing desert.

Critic's brand commercials 'carp puddles' or 'mud holes', but the fact is, today's mud hole is tomorrow's established fishery. Not everyone is fortunate enough to have the Severn, Great Ouse or Hampshire Avon at the bottom of their garden, or enjoy unfettered access to estate or syndicate lakes full of huge carp. It should be remembered many lapsed anglers packed in precisely because they were fed up scratching for bites on urban canals.

In our region we have some ultra hard canals, and the regularly polluted, but slowly recovering River Dee, while most of the big stillwaters are either owned by rich associations like Lymm, Warrington and Northwich, or rented by syndicates.

Personally, I'd love to fish the River Severn every week for barbel and chub.

For me though it means a 120 mile round trip, and given the cold water deluges, low summer levels, and then floods during the winter, I'd have to be sure the river was fishable, never mind in perfect condition, to justify the journey.

In contrast, commercial fisheries offer consistent all year round sport in a safe environment, where you are unlikely to be plagued by tackle thieves, bulls, big dogs and cows, nor end up playing tug of war with the neighbours over the back end of your pole! Where I do agree with the critics, is that for fishing to have any value there has to be the element of surprise. If every time the float goes under, you know it will be a two pound 'pastie carp' where is the magic? However, if fisheries have been created properly with plenty of bankside and underwater features, comfortable pegs, and a truly mixed stocking policy, they can provide the sort of sport and facilities I could only have dreamed of back in 1963.

One of the best, and most immaculately kept, is Border Fisheries near Crewe, where I had a surreal experience not long ago. Fishing the margins of the beautifully established and wooded Specimen lake with Ben, I lost a good carp, and a favourite float, when the line snapped just below the connector. A mere ten minutes later I hooked and landed another from the same swim, and low and behold, there was my float and rig still in its bottom lip! Who says fish feel pain and consequently shy away after a bad experience? Clearly the urge to eat transcends any sense of trepidation.

I do have some reservations though about commercially operated venues. Despite the universal insistence on barbless hooks, I note an increasing number of carp in pools where matches are staged several times a week (far too much) show signs of mouth damage.

I suspect this is down to barbless hooks slipping, as match anglers try to bully big fish to the net quickly, virtually dragging them through the water, as they ship the pole behind them so they can play it out on the top three. That technique should be banned.

Of course, just as there are both caring, and uncaring anglers, so there are good fishery owners and bad ones, including those who impose all sorts of ill-informed and sometimes ludicrous bans on methods and baits, like using someone else's branded pellets other than their own. I have even heard of flasks being banned, forcing people to buy tea from their café! The one that irritates me most though is the 'keepnet ban' which can be waived upon payment of an extra pound. So much for concern over the fish's welfare.

Along with Will Fair at Hampton Springs, one of the nicest fishery owners I have encountered is former Whiteacres owner Andy Seery, and his wife Debbie, who own and run the brilliant, and stunningly beautiful, Stafford Moor complex in north Devon. After using Whitacres as a base for two years, simply to get access to Bolingey and Gwinear, last summer we decided to switch our lads only fishing week to the north Devon venue, and hire two of Andy's magnificently appointed Scandinavian lodges for eight of us.

Though one dropped out, there was Chris, Garry (now a fully fledged policeman) and I in one lodge, and Jonesy, Cockney John, Ben and his mate, fireman John, in the other.

Unfortunately, this seemed to engender an unhealthy rivalry between the two lodges. They raided our fridge, so we filled their wellies with duck droppings!

The sport was superb though, with all the fish in immaculate condition, a testimony to sensible anglers, good fishery management and minimal bait bans. Rarely have I enjoyed such tranquillity and angling contentment. One afternoon, I had an entire eight-acre lake – the original one on the complex, now called Josephs – to myself, and caught a succession of quality roach, tench and carp, with just a curious roe deer for company.

On another lake, called 'Pines', I amassed a new personal best catch of 154lbs of carp, green and golden tench, crucians, roach and bream in just 6½ hours, leading Jonesy to bestow upon me yet another nickname – the 'pig of Pines'. Then in the resident's match, on Tanners, I set a new personal best match weight. Drawn on peg 9, I somehow came second with 66lbs 8ozs, taken on paste and pellet, which was enough to beat, by a couple of pounds, the cocky Cockney. Having stated he intended to "spank my scouse arse", he drew 'flyer' peg 35 and arrogantly announced, "Well, that's a result. Best angler, best peg!"

If he was somewhat dejected at being beaten by a 'Noddy' like me, he was utterly disconsolate when Jonesy weighed in an incredible 133lbs to set a new venue record for a resident match. The *best angler* finished fourth! Overall, Cockney John didn't have the best of weeks. One day, the platform upon which he was sitting collapsed and tipped him headfirst into the lake.

Chris meanwhile had chosen not to participate in the match, preferring to fish alone on Woodpecker lake, where casting a straight lead with banded pellet to the island, he had taken a huge net of carp to

9lbs odd. I went up to see him, as he was about to pack in.

"The carp are still queuing up out there," said Chris, firing another pouchful of pellets so they bounced off the island into the shallows. "Have a go yourself, the line is on the clip, so the lead will just hit the island and drop in."

Sitting on Chris's box, I took careful aim and cast towards the island, only for the lead to follow an entirely unexpected trajectory, and land in the one and only bush on that section of the island. Convulsed with laughter, Chris observed, "You're unbelievable. Do you know I've not snagged that bush once in nine hours fishing, yet you manage it with your first cast."

I bowed my head with shame. Despite the passage of 40 years since that first cast – and tangle – on the long lost 'Polo', some things in life never change!

Postscript

Less than a week after meeting publishers Sportsbooks Ltd, agreeing a contract, and handing over the final manuscript, serial fishing failure Peter Bishop, won his first ever fishing match, a club event, with 18lbs. 12ozs on a warm Sunday morning in May 2004.

In one of those strange quirks of fate, his modest winnings on the day would later be accompanied at the annual presentation night by a trophy, named in memory of local tackle dealer John A Parkes – the man who did much to inspire his passion for angling.

However, any suggestion that these two notable events were in some way connected and marked a watershed in Peter's angling fortunes has since been disproved.

Even his finest hour as a 'match' angler ended in another calamity. Having receiving a thunderous ovation from members and their partners at the club presentation night, Peter somehow managed to first juggle with, and then drop the solid silver cup and its base reducing everyone in the function room to fits of laughter!

Other books from SportsBooks

The Art of Bradman

Difficult to find a new book about the greatest batsman ever.
But this is unique. A selection of paintings of the great man from
the Bradman Museum at the Adelaide Oval with text by the
museum's curator.
Leatherbound with gold lettering and red ribbon marker.
ISBN 1899807 32 2
Price £25
Format 210mm x 280mm
Hardback
Pagination 240

Colin Blythe – lament for a legend

Chris Scoble
Colin Blythe was a giant in the golden age of county
cricket before the First World War. He was the most famous
England cricketer to be killed in the conflict. This is the first
biography of a complex personality, who was one of the
first cricketers to challenge the game's rulers, demanding to
handle his own financial affairs.
ISBN 1899807 31 4
Price £16.99
Format 154mm x 236mm
Hardback
Pagination 224

The Golf Majors 2005

Alun Evans
All the results and details of the game's premier tournaments,
the Masters, the British Open, the US Open and the PGA
Championships. The fourth edition of this book, but published

by SportsBooks for the first time. Paul Trow, of Golf World, called it "an invaluable source of information".
ISBN 1899807 24 1
Price £14.99
Format 138mm x 216mm
Paperback
Pagination 352

Athletics 2005

Editor Peter Matthews
The essential yearbook of the Association of Track & Field Statisticians and has been published every year since 1951. It contains details of the Athens Olympic Games. Previous annuals have been greatly prized by all true followers of the sport. Issues dating back to 1995 are also available.
ISBN 1899807 27 6
Price £17.95
Format 148mm x 210mm
Paperback
Pagination 608

The Rebel

Derek Roche - Irish warrior, British champion
Nigel McDermid
The tale of boxing hero Derek Roche is a journey from an Irish council estate to becoming the first Irishman to win a Lonsdale Belt outright. It also tells of Roche's days as a door-man in Leeds as he sought to earn a living outside the ring. The Irish Post called it a "modern classic". The Guardian said: "refreshingly honest and... genuinely funny".
ISBN 1899807 25 X
Price £7.99
Format 129mm x 198mm
Paperback
Pagination 240

Are You a Proper Teacher, Sir?
Gary Boothroyd
Twenty-seven years of teaching at an inner city
comprehensive school might sound like a life sentence to
some, but as Gary Boothroyd found out there was a lot of
fun to be had as well. His story encompasses the downright
hilarious and the occasional stark tragedy.
The Times Educational Supplement called it "a good light-
hearted read". The Yorkshire Evening Post said: "Ten out of
ten".
ISBN 1899807 26 8
Price £7.99
Format 129mm x 198mm
Paperback
Pagination 256

Test Cricket Grounds
John Woods
For dedicated cricket fans who plan to watch their country
play overseas. Woods spent a year and a day visiting all 58
grounds that stage Test cricket. Wisden International Cricket
magazine called it "a bible for the Barmy Army... perfect..."
ISBN 1899807 20 9
Price £12.99
Format 125mm x 217mm
Paperback
Pagination 480p all colour

Arthur Lydiard - Master Coach
Garth Gilmour
Arthur Lydiard was probably the most successful and influential
running coach of the twentieth century. Garth Gilmour, Lydiard's
close friend for more than 40 years, tells for the first time the
full story of the coach's amazing career, often in Lydiard's own
words.
Athletics Weekly said: "a perfect tribute to an immense genius".
ISBN 1899807 22 5

Price £17.99
Format 234mm x 153mm
Hardback
Pagination 256

International Rugby Who's Who

Andy Smith
This book provides all the fan needs to know about those
who play the game and coach at the top level from the
Zurich Premiership and Heineken Cup to the Super 12.
"An essential handbook... well produced," said the BBC.
ISBN 1899807 23 3
Price £17.95
Format 148mm x 210mm
Paperback
Pagination 428 all colour

The Complete Record of the FA Cup

Mike Collett
All you need to know about the oldest football club competition.
All the results from 1872, plus a 45,000 word history and facts
and figures to satisfy the most avid fan. The Independent called
it: "an awesome work of reference". The Guardian said it was:
"a masterwork". And Sky Sports called it: "unbelievable".
ISBN 1899807 19 5
Price £19.95
Format 148mm x 210mm
Paperback
Pagination 900

Raich Carter – the biography

Frank Garrick
Raich Carter is the only man to win FA Cup winners' medals
before and after the Second World War. Published to
commemorate the 10th anniversary of his death. The Times
said: "leaves the reader in no doubt about the nature of Carter's
genius".